The Essential Poets

*BOOK/CASSETTE PACKAGES AVAILABLE

Andrew Marvell

BORN   31 MARCH 1621
DIED   18 AUGUST 1678

The Essential
MARVELL

Selected and with an
Introduction by

DONALD HALL

The Ecco Press
New York

Introduction and selection copyright © 1991 by Donald Hall
All rights reserved
Published in 1991 by The Ecco Press
26 West 17th Street, New York, N.Y. 10011
Published simultaneously in Canada by
Penguin Books Canada Ltd., Ontario
Printed in the United States of America
Design by Reg Perry
FIRST EDITION

Library of Congress Cataloging-in-Publication Data
Marvell, Andrew, 1621–1678.
[Poems. Selections]
The essential Marvell
selected and with an introduction by Donald Hall.
p. cm.—(The Essential poets: v. 15)
Includes bibliographical references: $8.00
I. Hall, Donald, 1928– II. Title.
III. Series: Essential poets (New York, N.Y.): v. 15.
PR3546.A6   1991   821'.4—dc20   91-16899   CIP
ISBN 0-88001-312-5

Portrait of Andrew Marvell
Courtesy of the National Portrait Gallery,
London

Cassette recordings of live readings and interviews with
several of the series editors are available directly from
The Ecco Press in handsome book/cassette packages for $15.95
each. Call or write for details. Published by arrangement
with The Listening Library, Old Greenwich, CT. Jason Shinder,
general series interviewer and executive producer, is the
founder and director of The Writers' Voice, New York City.

Contents

❖❖

For Peter Davison

The Essential Marvell

Introduction

❖

Among the questions after a reading, people often ask, "Who's your favorite poet?" When I was young and sophisticated, I explained that I could not have one favorite; now I answer, "Thomas Hardy!" one day and "Marianne Moore!" the next—or, more often than not, "Andrew Marvell!" Only Marvell would have made the short list forty-five years ago and each year of all the years between. Of course the poetry has altered. Without a doubt, Marvell has produced much work, most especially "An Horatian Ode upon Cromwell's Return from Ireland," that only becomes accessible when we have read a little history. "Upon Appleton House" eluded us when we were young and lazy because of its length; now its length is luxury. But it is also true that the range and import of the old poems has enlarged: Their scale grows larger while their miniature size—pastoral conventions, *carpe diem*—remains the same.

The analogy of scale and size comes from sculpture, which provides another analogy: When we look at a bronze or stone Henry Moore "Reclining Figure," sited outside in a sculpture park, it changes as we walk around it. New lines of sight make new combinations, configurations, connections. If we continue to read a complex and multifaceted poem as we grow older, it alters each time we return to it. The greater the poem, the more it changes. We cannot read the same great poem twice. Thus, "To His Coy Mistress" veers over the years from flesh to bone. Universality gathers upon "The Garden" as youth's gregariousness proves shallow, and as solitude enhances meditation or the pleasures of imagination. Conviction of historical ambiguity, or of human diversity within the ostensibly single self, illuminates and deepens "An Horatian Ode upon Cromwell's Return from Ireland."

We know about Andrew Marvell's life because of his politics, not because of his poetry. He was a lively controversialist during the Restoration, satirizing the court from his republican vantage. He was also the dutiful and assiduous member of parliament who represented the city of Hull. What we know of Marvell's life frustrates us, for the poet inside the MP remains elusive.

The poet's father, also Andrew Marvell, was born in Meldreth eight miles south of Cambridge, educated at Emmanuel College, Cambridge, and in 1614 took the living at Winestead, in Holderness, where the poet was born seven years later. When Andrew *fils* was three years old, his father became preacher at Holy Trinity Church in Hull, as well as master of its grammar school; the poet was associated with the city for the rest of his life. (Three centuries later Philip Larkin lived and died there, librarian at the university.) Marvell's mother, whose name was Anne Pease, died in 1638, and his father remarried six months later—only to be drowned in 1640 while crossing the Humber. Thomas Fuller, who in his *Worthies* described the elder Marvell as "most facetious in his discourse, yet grave in his carriage," apportions blame: The preacher "drowned . . . by the carelessness (not to say drunkenness) of the boat-men."

Apparently father and son suffered a contretemps a year before the father drowned. It is believed that the poet left Trinity College, Cambridge (where he matriculated in 1633) in the company of Jesuits, a brief flirtation with the popery of which, as satirist, he became enemy. His father rooted him out of London—discovering him at a bookseller's—and brought him back to Trinity College and puritan values.

When Marvell went down from Trinity he spent some years traveling on the continent, possibly as a tutor, during the onset of the civil wars. He left England in 1642 and returned probably in 1646, master of Dutch, Italian, French, and Spanish. Presumably his Latin and Greek were in place before he left. He wrote many Latin poems; at least one

Greek poem survives. His Latin, both spoken and written, was fluent even for a 17th century man of learning; he employed his languages in office under Cromwell and later on diplomatic missions during the Restoration.

After he returned to England, Marvell tutored Mary Fairfax, daughter of a Cromwellian general who had left the field, at Appleton House in Yorkshire from 1650 to 1653. There he probably wrote much of his best poetry. Later John Milton (Latin Secretary to Cromwell; the office corresponded with foreign governments) recommended him to Cromwell as tutor for a ward of the Lord Protector living in Eton. Later still—in 1657—Marvell was appointed to assist Milton as Latin Secretary. (Another helper was the young John Dryden, many years later a royalist antagonist of Marvell.)

Marvell was first elected to parliament in 1660. Like his father, he was a moderate puritan, Church of England; yet like many other Cromwellians, he welcomed the Restoration, presumably for stability's sake. Marvell used his relative political security to free Milton from jail; it is possible that he saved Milton's life. Elected to parliament, he served his constituents until his death. Many of his letters to the Corporation of Hull are preserved in the Oxford University Press volumes of *Marvell's Poems and Letters,* meat for students of 17th century English political life. These official letters frequently lament that taxes must be raised. Private notes to his nephew William Popple contain gossip and even scurrilous jokes about the king; but Marvell was no fervent antiroyalist: He deplored courtly corruption but tolerated, or perhaps indulged, Charles the rake.

Marvell's political career was not without event. During his first session of parliament, he engaged in a public fistfight. From 1663 to 1665 he traveled on a trade embassy to Russia, with stops in Denmark and Sweden, an extraordinary adventure in the 17th century. Although we hear little about the journey in Marvell's own words, from other sources we understand that he was secretary to the mission and scripted letters home on behalf of the embassy's leader, the Earl of Carlisle. Czar Alexis professed dissatisfaction with Marvell's initial Latin address because Marvell called him "Illustrissimus" instead of "Serenissimus." The trip, which failed in its purpose, was a long series of aggravations. Early on, Marvell apparently pulled a gun on a recalcitrant teamster. Czar Alexis provided his English visitors a banquet that lasted for nine hours and consisted of 500 dishes. Marvell received the special attention of a sturgeon's head. We are told that the banquet ended only because the czar suffered a nosebleed.

In the last decade of his life, the public Marvell was quiet, representing Hull and reporting by regular letter to the corporation. Privately, or at any rate anonymously, Marvell was noisy: He occupied himself with political satire—anticourt, antipapist—in favor of toleration and liberty. When he died suddenly in 1678, perhaps of a stroke, it was rumored that Jesuits had poisoned him; he had recently satirized the church.

Marvell never married. After his death, his housekeeper Mary Palmer represented herself as Mary Marvell. As the poet's widow she stood to receive some monies owed the poet's estate. While he was alive, his political adversaries denounced Marvell as homosexual. Although his poems are full of pastoral love, no reader has ever discerned in his work tenderness toward a particular woman. The strongest erotic suggestion arises in "The Garden," where Marvell's vegetal eroticism exaggerates a convention. It is possible to read "The Definition of Love" as an ironic description of the difficulties of homosexual love. Maybe it provides a rueful account of unfulfilled homoerotic desire:

> As lines (so loves) oblique may well
> Themselves in every angle greet:
> But ours so truly parallel,
> Though infinite, can never meet.

But we only speculate.

Of his politics we may say more. From the start, Marvell was political. Who could be apolitical in the 17th century? From time to time he appears to stand on both sides of a question. His attack on the Cromwellian Tom May was written during Cromwell's time—when he also wrote Cromwellian panegyric. At the same time, one may discern consistencies in Marvell: He favored religious toleration, whether its opponents were low church or high; he attacked corruption in the Long parliament—and again in the court of Charles II. (Stories are told of Marvell's incorruptibility, of his refusal to take a bribe.) If he seems at times to stand on both sides of a question, we must ask how many issues limited themselves to two sides. The 17th century was politically many-sided, more complex than our age, and one need not have been the Vicar of Bray to appear inconsistent. To divide England into parties of "Cavalier" and "Roundhead" is to preclude understanding. One could stand to the parliament side on a dozen issues, and to the court side on a dozen others—at the same time, without inconsistency, much less hypocrisy.

Mixed loyalties were standard. Some rebels of the Long parliament considered themselves loyal subjects who wished to save the king from wicked advisors. (In retrospect, decapitation seems an extreme measure of correction.) Take Marvell's employer Fairfax, a great general for Cromwell against the king. (Milton himself addressed a sonnet to the parliamentary hero, "To My Lord Fairfax," ". . . whose name in arms through Europe rings . . .") Fairfax resigned his command when he disagreed with the Lord Protector; a Presbyterian himself, he would not invade Scotland. It was known that his wife was aghast at the execution of Charles I; it was rumored that Fairfax shared her opinion. Retired from combat, Fairfax returned to his country seat in Yorkshire, and later corresponded with Charles II from Appleton House. This old Cromwellian general helped to restore Charles II in 1660.

Ambivalence wove its texture into the details of all private and practical arrangements. The boy whom Marvell tutored at Eton—Cromwell's ward William Dutton—was son of a Cavalier who had died in 1646 in the royalist forces, but whose uncle arranged that William marry Cromwell's youngest daughter. Of course, when ambivalence tries to act, it finds itself incapable. That Cromwell's ward was royalist did not keep the king's head on his shoulders. To take part in the life of their times, Fairfax or Marvell or Milton needed perforce to take sides. From time to time, throughout his life, Marvell in his satires could sound dogmatic and single-minded. Only when he writes great poetry does Marvell's language embody ambivalence or manyness. If ambivalence makes for paralyzed politics and anarchic governance, it makes for poetry complex enough to mimic human complexity—and to be great.

It is a mark of Marvell's honorable manyness that, had he published the "Horatian Ode" in his lifetime, he would have been in trouble with both regicide and loyalist. He published little in his lifetime—poems printed in anthologies—and none of the poems for which we honor him. After his death, in 1681, his nephew William Popple issued *Miscellaneous Poems*. Only in small measure may we attribute this absence of publication to politics. Marvell was not a professional poet, as the young John Dryden was. Marvell's attitude toward himself as poet is old-fashioned; he resembles not Ben Jonson but Sir Walter Raleigh, or his own contemporary John Wilmot, Earl of Rochester, who was a poet among his other roles—gentleman and rake, for instance. Marvell was a poet, while he was also a tutor, Latinist, bureaucrat, and MP.

Marvell was also old-fashioned in poetic style, which helps to account for the strange history of his reputation. Usually he hoed his tetrameter garden, instead of going avant-garde with the heroic couplet that Dryden spent his life exploring and extending. Marvell also cultivated the old metaphoric extravagance associated with John Donne, the out-of-fashion, faintly fusty metaphysical style. To someone reading his work late in the 17th century, Marvell must have seemed reactionary—

like Thomas Hardy writing rhymed lyrics in the heyday of 1920s modernism.

When Popple published *Miscellaneous Poems,* no one celebrated a great poet. For that matter, readers lacked his greatest work: "An Horatian Ode" was suppressed until a century after Marvell's death. Popple at first seems to have included it; this poem and the lesser work on Cromwell's death turn up in two surviving copies; in all other copies they have been removed. It was not until 1776 that Marvell's Cromwellian poems reached print.

Meanwhile, Marvell the lyric poet lacked an audience. When English booksellers chose poets as subjects for Samuel Johnson's biographies, Marvell's name went unlisted; it would not have occurred to anyone. Other 17th century poets, like Robert Herrick and Thomas Campion, also remained forgotten until the romantics found them, but Marvell had the misfortune to be remembered for something other than his poetry. All through the 18th century, his was a name for Whigs and lovers of liberty to conjure with. Jonathan Swift praised and learned from Marvell's satirical prose, especially *The Rehearsal Transpros'd.* When William Wordsworth thought of Marvell it was as a son of liberty: "Great men have been among us . . . Sydney, Marvell, Harrington."

It took a later generation of romantics to discover the poetry. At first they considered him merely a poet of nature, but once he was reprinted, the discovery could expand. The antiquarian Charles Lamb found him, read him, and praised him. William Hazlitt reprinted some of the best work in an 1825 collection. Francis Palgrave treasuried him. Alfred, Lord Tennyson recited him to friends. T. H. Ward's *English Poets* (1880) left out "To His Coy Mistress" (perhaps as distressing in 1880 as praise for Cromwell in 1681) but printed "An Horatian Ode," "Bermudas," and "The Garden."

One would think the battle won. But if we had learned to admire the poetry, we had not credited its greatness. When Augustine Birrell wrote about Marvell in 1905, for the "English Men of Letters" series, he was limited in his praise. "A finished master of his art," Birrell says, "he never was." He compares Marvell's skill unfavorably with the poetry of Richard Lovelace, Abraham Cowley, and Edmund Waller. "He is often clumsy," Birrell writes, "and sometimes almost babyish."

In 1922 the Oxford University Press published *Andrew Marvell,* tercentenary tributes by eight critics, including mossbacks like Edmund Gosse and J.C. Squire—and the Young Turk T.S. Eliot. We can consult this volume to read the "Tercentenary Sermon" at Holy Trinity Church and the "Tercentenary Address" at the Guild Hall in Hull, or to read about "The Marvell Tramcars" and study photographs of a Hull trolley repainted in honor of the city's poet and parliamentarian. Of course, it is Eliot's great essay, reprinted from the *Times Literary Supplement,* that especially fixed our attentions on Marvell's excellence: neglected for two centuries, condescended to for another.

When you love a poet's poems, it is annoying to feel required to adduce reasons. But if you are to move a skeptic, you need to try. One can cite touchstones. For a hundred years people have used

> *Annihilating all that's made*
> *To a green thought in a green shade*

as an example of poetry or even of the poetic. In the 17th century I am sure that this couplet was an example of wit; by history's revisionary magic, two centuries later its wit vanished in romantic smoke. Its thoughtful trope—an exaggeration of concentration, the inward defining itself as outward—came to seem mystic: a moment of pantheistic ego-loss or Freud's oceanic feeling.

Why not both at once?

Surely this couplet is poetry at its most condensed. Marvell was expert at loading every rift with ore. A rift loaded with ore is never mere quantity; rifts are most loaded when number is not so much dense as various. The smoothly rolling polysyllabic Latin of "annihilating," with its densely syntaxed accusative Anglish monosyllabic "all that's made," contrasts with (and completes itself in) a monosyllabic line absolutely balanced—preposition/article/adjective/noun, preposition/article/adjective/noun—in which four out of eight monosyllables appear twice. Wit and grammar together embody the pleasurable, mildly scary obscuration of consciousness, both at once. Three hundred years of consciousness about consciousness hook together in these lines.

Marvell's banner reads, *both at once*. The simultaneous affirmation of opposing forces—by no means limited to two items—requires compression. By this compression we not only acknowledge ambivalence, we embody it.

His couplets accommodate a vast range of tone and of pacing. If the beginning of "To His Coy Mistress" is old-fashioned and metaphysical—hyperbolically witty, slow in its performance of slowness—the end of the poem is modern, streamlined, and speeds like nothing else in English poetry: and all, perforce, to the same octosyllabic tune. Barbara Everett refers to "An Horatian Ode" when she observes that "Marvell is using a metre for thinking aloud in"—but in his great poems he always uses meter to think aloud in. The tetrameter couplet balanced four against four, and each four balanced two against two—except when eccentric caesura saw that it didn't, which was shocking or outrageous:

> *Thus, though we cannot make our sun*
> *Stand still, yet we will make him run.*

Poetry is a language for thinking aloud in—and not for putting thoughts into words, although the philosophical heresy is almost universal among critics. (Everett is an exception.) Metaphor, syntax, image, meter, and rhythm are means of thought; so is overall construction. "To His Coy Mistress" has been well-observed: its logical structure, its combinations of flesh and bone, time and space, eros and thanatos, its use of poetic conventions 2,000 years old. It is the culminating poem of a millenial sequence that affirms: *Make love because you die.* In the process, this theme combines in one poem the two subjects of human discourse—both at once.

Poetry exists to say and do *both at once.* Philosophical discourse dedicates itself to find, to set forth, and to decide what's first or best or true. Only poetry admits (proclaims, insists, shouts), *Both at once!* or even, *All at once!* (therefore, I need call Heraclitus, Emerson, and Nietszche poets)—not only Marvell's but surely Marvell is foremost among the manysayers. Manyness is ineluctibly human, and poetry (among human artifacts) best embodies manyness.

Although we need from time to time to make a choice—Marvell voted, Marvell advocated and denounced—choices are always *faute de mieux.* To pretend otherwise is to lie, an activity deplored by the Muse. Utterly captured by the mixed political life of 17th century England, housed with many-sided Fairfax at Nun Appleton, Marvell found in the expression of ambivalence his poetic form and power.

If Marvell made the octosyllabic couplet his own, using the modern pentameter couplet only for lighter work, he experimented in his greatest single work to marry the tetrameter couplet to a trimeter, constructing the eloquent, heartbreaking stanza of "An Horatian Ode." The Cromwell who appears in Marvell's poem is massive, violent, and willful:

> *Then burning through the air he went,*
> *And palaces and temples rent:*
>   *And Caesar's head at last*
>   *Did through his laurels blast.*

The last line trembles the scale, as we sort its syntax out and watch "blast" perform its possibilities. We must reconstruct Marvell's Cromwell away from normative leaders like Napoleon and Hitler, who have been praised in similar terms, because:

> Much to the man is due
> Who, from his private gardens, where
> He lived reservèd and austere,
>   As if his highest plot
>   To plant the bergamot,
> Could by industrious valour climb
> To ruin the great work of time,
>   And cast the kingdoms old
>   Into another mould.

Meter, consonants, and syntax mimic strength, embody phallic masculine muscularity and determination. In the great couplet, "Could by industrious valour climb / To ruin the great work of time," Marvell clearly values both "valour" and "the great work." Emotions conflict, values conflict, and "valour" destroys "great work" as an army lays waste to a castle. I think of Yeats' oxymoron, "terrible beauty," in "Easter, 1916"—where the words "is born" give narrow victory to beauty over terror.

Marvell the traditionalist poet is not unmoved by tradition. The poem continues:

> Though justice against fate complain,
> And plead the ancient rights in vain:
>   But those do hold or break
>   As men are strong or weak.
> Nature, that hateth emptiness,
> Allows of penetration less:
>   And therefore must make room
>   Where greater spirits come.

The most eloquent and touching stanzas describe the execution of Charles, written by the poet later described by royalists as a "bitter republican."

> *He nothing common did or mean*
> *Upon that memorable scene:*
>   *But with his keener eye*
>   *The axe's edge did try:*
> *Nor called the gods with vulgar spite*
> *To vindicate his helpless right,*
>   *But bowed his comely head,*
>   *Down, as upon a bed.*

Everett remarks "Everything is beautiful, and something is betrayed." There is nothing greater in English poetry than this beautiful betrayal— but Marvell does not end with this passage, which would have ended most poets' poems. Praise for Cromwell continues to find glory in the power, and yet the poem ends in a prophetic aside that shades itself back over the 118 lines before.

> *The same arts that did gain*
> *A power, must it maintain.*

The poise of Marvell's judgment waivers, but it concludes, as it does in his great poems, with an appropriately complex justice. Such conclusions are neither simple nor comforting—except that the existence of honest, difficult human intelligence consoles us: Poetry's thinking consoles us.

A note on other editions and other reading:

Few biographers have undertaken a life of Andrew Marvell. Look at John Dixon Hunt's *Andrew Marvell* (Cornell University Press, 1978). In the 20th century there are many essays, notably T. S. Eliot's from

1921 (*Selected Essays,* Harcourt Brace Jovanovich). Look at Philip Larkin's "The Changing Face of Andrew Marvell" in Larkin's *Required Writing* (Farrar, Straus & Giroux, 1984); the librarian from Hull is lucid and summary about the MP for Hull. The best essay is Barbara Everett's "The Shooting of the Bears: Poetry and Politics in Andrew Marvell," in her *Poets in Their Times* (Faber & Faber, 1986).

Texts for poems and letters will be found in H.M. Margoliouth's two volumes from the Oxford University Press, currently in a third edition revised, after Margoliouth's death, by Pierre Legouis and E.E. Duncan-Jones. For our text I have relied on the Penguin Classics edition intelligently edited by Elizabeth Story Donno. She has modernized spelling and typography. When I choose to differ with her readings, I have noted it.

— DONALD HALL

Poems

❖❖

A Dialogue between Thyrsis and Dorinda

DORINDA
When death shall part us from these kids,
And shut up our divided lids,
Tell me, Thyrsis, prithee do,
Whither thou and I must go.

THYRSIS
To the Elysium.

DORINDA
            Oh, where is't?

THYRSIS
A chaste soul can never miss't.

DORINDA
I know no way but to our home,
Is our cell Elysium?

THYRSIS
Turn thine eye to yonder sky,
There the milky way doth lie;
'Tis a sure but rugged way,
That leads to everlasting day.

DORINDA

There birds may nest, but how can I
That have no wings and cannot fly?

THYRSIS

Do not sigh, fair nymph, for fire
Hath no wings yet doth aspire
Till it hit against the Pole:
Heaven's the centre of the soul.

DORINDA

But in Elysium how do they
Pass eternity away?

THYRSIS

Oh, there's neither hope nor fear,
There's no wolf, no fox, no bear.
No need of dog to fetch our stray,
Our Lightfoot we may give away;
No oat-pipe's needful; there thy ears
May sleep with music of the spheres.

DORINDA

Oh sweet! Oh sweet! How I my future state
By silent thinking antedate:
I prithee let us spend our time to come
In talking of Elysium.

THYRSIS

Then I'll go on. There sheep are full
Of sweetest grass and softest wool;
There birds sing consorts, garlands grow,
Cool winds do whisper, springs do flow.
There always is a rising sun,

And day is ever but begun.
Shepherds there bear equal sway,
And every nymph's a Queen of May.

DORINDA
Ah me, ah me!

THYRSIS
           Dorinda, why dost cry?

DORINDA
I'm sick, I'm sick, and fain would die.
Convince me now that this is true
By bidding with me all adieu.

THYRSIS
I cannot live without thee, I,
I'll for thee, much more with thee, die.

CHORUS
Then let us give Corillo charge o' the sheep,
And thou and I'll pick poppies, and them steep
In wine, and drink on't even till we weep,
So shall we smoothly pass away in sleep.

A Dialogue, between the Resolved Soul and Created Pleasure

Courage, my Soul, now learn to wield
The weight of thine immortal shield.
Close on thy head thy helmet bright.
Balance thy sword against the fight.
See where an army, strong as fair,
With silken banners spreads the air.

Now, if thou be'st that thing divine,
In this day's combat let it shine:
And show that Nature wants an art
To conquer one resolvèd heart.

PLEASURE
Welcome the creation's guest,
Lord of earth, and heaven's heir.
Lay aside that warlike crest,
And of Nature's banquet share:
Where the souls of fruits and flowers
Stand prepared to heighten yours.

SOUL
I sup above, and cannot stay
To bait so long upon the way.

PLEASURE
On these downy pillows lie,
Whose soft plumes will thither fly:
On these roses strewed so plain
Lest one leaf thy side should strain.

SOUL
My gentler rest is on a thought,
Conscious of doing what I ought.

PLEASURE
If thou be'st with perfumes pleased,
Such as oft the gods appeased,
Thou in fragrant clouds shalt show
Like another god below.

SOUL

A soul that knows not to presume
Is heaven's and its own perfume.

PLEASURE

Everything does seem to vie
Which should first attract thine eye:
But since none deserves that grace,
In this crystal view *thy* face.

SOUL

When the Creator's skill is prized,
The rest is all but earth disguised.

PLEASURE

Hark how music then prepares
For thy stay these charming airs;
Which the posting winds recall,
And suspend the river's fall.

SOUL

Had I but any time to lose,
On this I would it all dispose.
Cease, tempter. None can chain a mind
Whom this sweet chordage cannot bind.

CHORUS

Earth cannot show so brave a sight
As when a single soul does fence
The batteries of alluring sense,
And heaven views it with delight.
   Then persevere: for still new charges sound:
   And if thou overcom'st, thou shalt be crowned.

PLEASURE

All this fair, and soft, and sweet,
    Which scatteringly doth shine,
Shall within one beauty meet,
    And she be only thine.

SOUL

If things of sight such heavens be,
What heavens are those we cannot see?

PLEASURE

Wheresoe'er thy foot shall go
    The minted gold shall lie,
Till thou purchase all below,
    And want new worlds to buy.

SOUL

Were't not a price, who'd value gold?
And that's worth naught that can be sold.

PLEASURE

Wilt thou all the glory have
    That war or peace commend?
Half the world shall be thy slave
    The other half thy friend.

SOUL

What friends, if to my self untrue!
What slaves, unless I captive you!

PLEASURE

Thou shalt know each hidden cause;
    And see the future time:

Try what depth the centre draws;
   And then to heaven climb.

SOUL

None thither mounts by the degree
Of knowledge, but humility.

CHORUS

Triumph, triumph, victorious Soul;
The world has not one pleasure more:
The rest does lie beyond the Pole,
And is thine everlasting store.

Flecknoe, an English Priest at Rome

Obliged by frequent visits of this man,
Whom as priest, poet, and musician,
I for some branch of Melchizédek took
(Though he derives himself from my Lord Brooke);
I sought his lodging, which is at the sign
Of The Sad Pelican—subject divine
For poetry. There, three staircases high—
Which signifies his triple property—
I found at last a chamber, as 'twas said,
But seemed a coffin set on the stairs' head
Not higher than seven, nor larger than three feet;
Only there was nor ceiling, nor a sheet,
Save that the ingenious door did, as you come,
Turn in, and show to wainscot half the room.
Yet of his state no man could have complained,
There being no bed where he entertained:
And though within one cell so narrow pent,
He'd stanzas for a whole *apartément*.

Straight without further information,
In hideous verse, he, in a dismal tone,
Begins to exorcise, as if I were
Possessed; and sure the Devil brought me there.
But I, who now imagined myself brought
To my last trial, in a serious thought
Calmed the disorders of my youthful breast,
And to my martyrdom preparèd rest.
Only this frail ambition did remain,
The last distemper of the sober brain,
That there had been some present to assure
The future ages how I did endure:
And how I, silent, turned my burning ear
Towards the verse; and when that could not hear,
Held him the other; and unchangèd yet,
Asked still for more, and prayed him to repeat:
Till the tyrant, weary to persecute,
Left off, and tried to allure me with his lute.

Now as two instruments, to the same key
Being tuned by art, if the one touchèd be
The other opposite as soon replies,
Moved by the air and hidden sympathies;
So while he with his gouty fingers crawls
Over the lute, his murm'ring belly calls,
Whose hungry guts to the same straitness twined
In echo to the trembling strings repined.

I, that perceived now what his music meant,
Asked civilly if he had eat this Lent.
He answered yes, with such and such an one.
For he has this of generous, that alone
He never feeds, save only when he tries
With gristly tongue to dart the passing flies.
I asked if he eat flesh. And he, that was
So hungry that, though ready to say Mass,

Would break his fast before, said he was sick,
And the ordinance was only politic.
Nor was I longer to invite him scant,
Happy at once to make him Protestant,
And silent. Nothing now our dinner stayed
But till he had himself a body made—
I mean till he were dressed: for else so thin
He stands, as if he only fed had been
With consecrated wafers: and the Host
Hath sure more flesh and blood than he can boast.
This *basso relievo* of a man,
Who as a camel tall, yet easily can
The needle's eye thread without any stitch,
(His only impossible is to be rich),
Lest his too subtle body, growing rare,
Should leave his soul to wander in the air,
He therefore circumscribes himself in rimes;
And swaddled in's own papers seven times,
Wears a close jacket of poetic buff,
With which he doth his third dimension stuff.
Thus armèd underneath, he over all
Does make a primitive *sottana* fall;
And above that yet casts an antique cloak,
Torn at the first Council of Antioch,
Which by the Jews long hid, and disesteemed,
He heard of by tradition, and redeemed.
But were he not in this black habit decked,
This half-transparent man would soon reflect
Each colour that he passed by, and be seen,
As the chameleon, yellow, blue, or green.

   He dressed, and ready to disfurnish now
His chamber, whose compactness did allow
No empty place for complimenting doubt,
But who came last is forced first to go out;

I meet one on the stairs who made me stand,
Stopping the passage, and did him demand.
I answered, 'He is here, Sir; but you see
You cannot pass to him but thorough me.'
He thought himself affronted, and replied,
'I whom the palace never has denied
Will make the way here;' I said, 'Sir, you'll do
Me a great favour, for I seek to go.'
He gathering fury still made sign to draw;
But himself there closed in a scabbard saw
As narrow as his sword's; and I, that was
Delightful, said, 'There can no body pass
Except by penetration hither, where
Two make a crowd; nor can three persons here
Consist but in one substance.' Then, to fit
Our peace, the priest said I too had some wit.
To prov't, I said, 'The place doth us invite
By its own narrowness, Sir, to unite.'
He asked me pardon; and to make me way
Went down, as I him followed to obey.
But the propitiatory priest had straight
Obliged us, when below, to celebrate
Together our atonement: so increased
Betwixt us two the dinner to a feast.

Let it suffice that we could eat in peace;
And that both poems did and quarrels cease
During the table; though my new-made friend
Did, as he threatened, ere 'twere long intend
To be both witty and valiant: I, loath,
Said 'twas too late, he was already both.

But now, alas, my first tormentor came,
Who satisfied with eating, but not tame,
Turns to recite; though judges most severe
After the assize's dinner mild appear,

And on full stomach do condemn but few,
Yet he more strict my sentence doth renew,
And draws out of the black box of his breast
Ten quire of paper in which he was dressed.
Yet that which was a greater cruelty
Than Nero's poem, he calls charity:
And so the pelican at his door hung
Picks out the tender bosom to its young.
    Of all his poems there he stands ungirt
Save only two foul copies for his shirt:
Yet these he promises as soon as clean.
But how I loathed to see my neighbour glean
Those papers which he peelèd from within
Like white flakes rising from a leper's skin!
More odious than those rags which the French youth
At ordinaries after dinner show'th
When they compare their chancres and poulains.
Yet he first kissed them, and after takes pains
To read; and then, because he understood
Not one word, thought and swore that they were good.
But all his praises could not now appease
The provoked author, whom it did displease
To hear his verses, by so just a curse,
That were ill made, condemned to be read, worse:
And how (impossible) he made yet more
Absurdities in them than were before.
For he his untuned voice did fall or raise
As a deaf man upon a viol plays,
Making the half points and the periods run
Confuseder than the atoms in the sun.
Thereat the poet swelled, with anger full,
And roared out, like Perillus in's own bull:
'Sir, you read false.' 'That, any one but you,
Should know the contrary.' Whereat, I, now

Made mediator, in my room, said, 'Why,
To say that you read false, Sir, is no lie.'
Thereat the waxen youth relented straight;
But saw with sad despair that 'twas too late.
For the disdainful poet was retired
Home, his most furious satire to have fired
Against the rebel, who, at this struck dead,
Wept bitterly as disinherited.
Who should commend his mistress now? Or who
Praise him? Both difficult indeed to do
With truth. I counselled him to go in time,
Ere the fierce poet's anger turned to rime.
    He hasted; and I, finding myself free,
As one 'scaped strangely from captivity,
Have made the chance be painted; and go now
To hang it in Saint Peter's for a vow.

The Fair Singer

1

To make a final conquest of all me,
Love did compose so sweet an enemy,
In whom both beauties to my death agree,
Joining themselves in fatal harmony;
    That while she with her eyes my heart does bind,
    She with her voice might captivate my mind.

2

I could have fled from one but singly fair:
My disentangled soul itself might save,
Breaking the curlèd trammels of her hair;
But how should I avoid to be her slave,

Whose subtle art invisibly can wreathe
My fetters of the very air I breathe?

3

It had been easy fighting in some plain,
Where victory might hang in equal choice.
But all resistance against her is vain,
Who has the advantage both of eyes and voice,
And all my forces needs must be undone,
She having gainèd both the wind and sun.

The Gallery

1

Clora, come view my soul, and tell
Whether I have contrived it well.
Now all its several lodgings lie
Composed into one gallery;
And the great arras-hangings, made
Of various faces, by are laid;
That, for all furniture, you'll find
Only your picture in my mind.

2

Here thou are painted in the dress
Of an inhuman murderess;
Examining upon our hearts
Thy fertile shop of cruel arts:
Engines more keen than ever yet
Adorned a tyrant's cabinet;
Of which the most tormenting are
Black eyes, red lips, and curlèd hair.

3

But, on the other side, th'art drawn
Like to Aurora in the dawn;
When in the East she slumbering lies,
And stretches out her milky thighs;
While all the morning choir does sing,
And manna falls, and roses spring;
And, at thy feet, the wooing doves
Sit pérfecting their harmless loves.

4

Like an enchantress here thou show'st,
Vexing thy restless lover's ghost;
And, by a light obscure, dost rave
Over his entrails, in the cave;
Divining thence, with horrid care,
How long thou shalt continue fair;
And (when informed) them throw'st away,
To be the greedy vulture's prey.

5

But, against that, thou sit'st afloat
Like Venus in her pearly boat.
The halcyons, calming all that's nigh,
Betwixt the air and water fly;
Or, if some rolling wave appears,
A mass of ambergris it bears.
Nor blows more wind than what may well
Convoy the perfume to the smell.

6

These pictures and a thousand more
Of thee my gallery do store
In all the forms thou canst invent

Either to please me, or torment:
For thou alone to people me,
Art grown a numerous colony;
And a collection choicer far
Than or Whitehall's or Mantua's were.

7

But, of these pictures and the rest,
That at the entrance likes me best:
Where the same posture, and the look
Remains, with which I first was took:
A tender shepherdess, whose hair
Hangs loosely playing in the air,
Transplanting flowers from the green hill,
To crown her head, and bosom fill.

The Unfortunate Lover

1

Alas, how pleasant are their days
With whom the infant Love yet plays!
Sorted by pairs, they still are seen
By fountains cool, and shadows green.
But soon these flames do lose their light,
Like meteors of a summer's night:
Nor can they to that region climb,
To make impression upon time.

2

'Twas in a shipwreck, when the seas
Ruled, and the winds did what they please,
That my poor lover floating lay,
And, ere brought forth, was cast away:

Till at the last the master-wave
Upon the rock his mother drave;
And there she split against the stone,
In a Caesarean séctión.

3

The sea him lent those bitter tears
Which at his eyes he always wears;
And from the winds the sighs he bore,
Which through his surging breast do roar.
No day he saw but that which breaks
Through frighted clouds in forkèd streaks,
While round the rattling thunder hurled,
As at the funeral of the world.

4

While Nature to his birth presents
This masque of quarrelling elements,
A numerous fleet of cormorants black,
That sailed insulting o'er the wrack,
Received into their cruel care
Th' unfortunate and abject heir:
Guardians most fit to entertain
The orphan of the hurricane.

5

They fed him up with hopes and air,
Which soon digested to despair,
And as one cormorant fed him, still
Another on his heart did bill,
Thus while they famish him, and feast,
He both consumèd, and increased:
And languishèd with doubtful breath,
The amphibíum of life and death.

6

And now, when angry heaven would
Behold a spectacle of blood,
Fortune and he are called to play
At sharp before it all the day:
And tyrant Love his breast does ply
With all his winged artillery,
Whilst he, betwixt the flames and waves,
Like Ajax, the mad tempest braves.

7

See how he nak'd and fierce does stand,
Cuffing the thunder with one hand,
While with the other he does lock,
And grapple, with the stubborn rock:
From which he with each wave rebounds,
Torn into flames, and ragg'd with wounds,
And all he 'says, a lover dressed
In his own blood does relish best.

8

This is the only banneret
That ever Love created yet:
Who though, by the malignant stars,
Forcèd to live in storms and wars,
Yet dying leaves a perfume here,
And music within every ear:
And he in story only rules,
In a field sable a lover gules.

Daphnis and Chloe

1

Daphnis must from Chloe part:
Now is come the dismal hour
That must all his hopes devour,
All his labour, all his art.

2

Nature, her own sex's foe,
Long had taught her to be coy:
But she neither knew t'enjoy,
Nor yet let her lover go.

3

But with this sad news surprised,
Soon she let that niceness fall,
And would gladly yield to all,
So it had his stay comprised.

4

Nature so herself does use
To lay by her wonted state,
Lest the world should separate;
Sudden parting closer glues.

5

He, well-read in all the ways
By which men their siege maintain,
Knew not that the fort to gain,
Better 'twas the siege to raise.

6

But he came so full possessed
With the grief of parting thence,
That he had not so much sense
As to see he might be blessed.

7

Till Love in her language breathed
Words she never spake before,
But than legacies no more
To a dying man bequeathed.

8

For, alas, the time was spent,
Now the latest minute's run
When poor Daphnis is undone,
Between joy and sorrow rent.

9

At that 'Why', that 'Stay, my Dear',
His disordered locks he tare;
And with rolling eyes did glare,
And his cruel fate forswear.

10

As the soul of one scarce dead,
With the shrieks of friends aghast,
Looks distracted back in haste,
And then straight again is fled,

11

So did wretched Daphnis look,
Frighting her he lovèd most.

At the last, this lover's ghost
Thus his leave resolvèd took.

12

'Are my hell and heaven joined
More to torture him that dies?
Could departure not suffice,
But that you must then grow kind?

13

'Ah, my Chloe, how have I
Such a wretched minute found,
When thy favours should me wound
More than all thy cruelty?

14

'So to the condemnèd wight
The delicious cup we fill;
And allow him all he will,
For his last and short delight.

15

'But I will not now begin
Such a debt unto my foe;
Nor to my departure owe
What my presence could not win.

16

'Absence is too much alone:
Better 'tis to go in peace,
Than my losses to increase
By a late fruition.

17

'Why should I enrich my fate?
'Tis a vanity to wear,
For my executioner,
Jewels of so high a rate.

18

'Rather I away will pine
In a manly stubborness
Than be fatted up express
For the cannibal to dine.

19

'Whilst this grief does thee disarm,
All th' enjoyment of our love
But the ravishment would prove
Of a body dead while warm.

20

'And I parting should appear
Like the gourmand Hebrew dead,
While with quails and manna fed,
He does through the desert err.

21

'Or the witch that midnight wakes
For the fern, whose magic weed
In one minute casts the seed,
And invisible him makes.

22

'Gentler times for love are meant:
Who for parting pleasure strain

Gather roses in the rain,
Wet themselves, and spoil their scent.

23

'Farewell, therefore, all the fruit
Which I could from love receive:
Joy will not with sorrow weave,
Nor will I this grief pollute.

24

'Fate, I come, as dark, as sad,
As thy malice could desire;
Yet bring with me all the fire
That Love in his torches had.'

25

At these words away he broke;
As who long has praying li'n,
To his headsman makes the sign,
And receives the parting stroke.

26

But hence, virgins, all beware:
Last night he with Phlogis slept;
This night for Dorinda kept;
And but rid to take the air.

27

Yet he does himself excuse;
Nor indeed without a cause:
For, according to the laws,
Why did Chloe once refuse?

Upon the Death of the Lord Hastings

Go, intercept some fountain in the vein,
Whose virgin-source yet never steeped the plain.
Hastings is dead, and we must find a store
Of tears untouched, and never wept before.
Go, stand betwixt the morning and the flowers;
And, ere they fall, arrest the early showers.
Hastings is dead; and we, disconsolate,
With early tears must mourn his early fate.

Alas, his virtues did his death presage:
Needs must he die, that doth out-run his age.
The phlegmatic and slow prolongs his day,
And on Time's wheel sticks like a remora.
What man is he that hath not heaven beguiled,
And is not thence mistaken for a child?
While those of growth more sudden, and more bold,
Are hurried hence, as if already old.
For, there above, they number not as here,
But weigh to man the geometric year.

Had he but at this measure still increased,
And on the Tree of Life once made a feast,
As that of Knowledge; what loves had he given
To earth, and then what jealousies to heaven!
But 'tis a maxim of that state, that none,
Lest he become like them, taste more than one.
Therefore the democratic stars did rise,
And all that worth from hence did ostracize.

Yet as some prince, that, for state-jealousy,
Secures his nearest and most loved ally;
His thought with richest triumphs entertains,
And in the choicest pleasures charms his pains:
So he, not banished hence, but there confined,
There better recreates his active mind.

Before the crystal palace where he dwells,
The armèd angels hold their carousels;
And underneath, he views the tournaments
Of all these sublunary elements.
But most he doth the Eternal Book behold,
On which the happy names do stand enrolled;
And gladly there can all his kindred claim,
But most rejoices at his Mother's name.

    The gods themselves cannot their joy conceal,
But draw their veils, and their pure beams reveal:
Only they drooping Hymeneus note,
Who, for sad purple, tears his saffron coat;
And trails his torches through the starry hall
Reversèd at his darling's funeral.
And Aesculapius, who, ashamed and stern,
Himself at once condemneth, and Mayern
Like some sad chemist, who, prepared to reap
The golden harvest, sees his glasses leap.
For, how immortal must their race have stood,
Had Mayern once been mixed with Hastings' blood!
How sweet and verdant would these laurels be,
Had they been planted on that balsam tree!

    But what could he, good man, although he bruised
All herbs, and them a thousand ways infused?
All he had tried, but all in vain, he saw,
And wept, as we, without redress or law.
For man (alas) is but the heaven's sport;
And art indeed is long, but life is short.

The Definition of Love

1

My love is of a birth as rare
As 'tis for object strange and high:
It was begotten by Despair
Upon Impossibility.

2

Magnanimous Despair alone
Could show me so divine a thing,
Where feeble Hope could ne'er have flown
But vainly flapped its tinsel wing.

3

And yet I quickly might arrive
Where my extended soul is fixed,
But Fate does iron wedges drive,
And always crowds itself betwixt.

4

For Fate with jealous eye does see
Two perfect loves, nor lets them close:
Their union would her ruin be,
And her tyrannic power depose.

5

And therefore her decrees of steel
Us as the distant Poles have placed,
(Though Love's whole world on us doth wheel)
Not by themselves to be embraced,

Unless the giddy heaven fall,
And earth some new convulsion tear;
And, us to join, the world should all
Be cramped into a planisphere.

7

As lines (so loves) oblique may well
Themselves in every angle greet:
But ours so truly parallel,
Though infinite, can never meet.

Therefore the love which us doth bind,
But Fate so enviously debars,
Is the conjunction of the mind,
And opposition of the stars.

To His Coy Mistress

Had we but world enough, and time,
This coyness, Lady, were no crime.
We would sit down, and think which way
To walk, and pass our long love's day.
Thou by the Indian Ganges' side
Shouldst rubies find: I by the tide
Of Humber would complain. I would
Love you ten years before the flood:
And you should, if you please, refuse
Till the conversion of the Jews.
My vegetable love should grow
Vaster than empires, and more slow.
An hundred years should go to praise

Thine eyes, and on thy forehead gaze.
Two hundred to adore each breast:
But thirty thousand to the rest.
An age at least to every part,
And the last age should show your heart:
For, Lady, you deserve this state;
Nor would I love at lower rate.

But at my back I always hear
Time's wingèd chariot hurrying near:
And yonder all before us lie
Deserts of vast eternity.
Thy beauty shall no more be found;
Nor, in thy marble vault, shall sound
My echoing song: then worms shall try
That long-preserved virginity:
And your quaint honour turn to dust;
And into ashes all my lust.
The grave's a fine and private place,
But none, I think, do there embrace.

Now, therefore, while the youthful hue
Sits on thy skin like morning dew,
And while thy willing soul transpires
At every pore with instant fires,
Now let us sport us while we may;
And now, like amorous birds of prey,
Rather at once our time devour,
Than languish in his slow-chapped power.
Let us roll all our strength, and all
Our sweetness, up into one ball:
And tear our pleasures with rough strife,
Thorough the iron gates of life.
Thus, though we cannot make our sun
Stand still, yet we will make him run.

Eyes and Tears

1

How wisely Nature did decree,
With the same eyes to weep and see!
That, having viewed the object vain,
We might be ready to complain.

2

Thus since the self-deluding sight,
In a false angle takes each height,
These tears, which better measure all,
Like watery lines and plummets fall.

3

Two tears, which Sorrow long did weigh
Within the scales of either eye,
And then paid out in equal poise,
Are the true price of all my joys.

4

What in the world most fair appears,
Yea, even laughter, turns to tears:
And all the jewels which we prize,
Melt in these pendants of the eyes.

5

I have through every garden been,
Amongst the red, the white, the green,
And yet, from all the flowers I saw,
No honey but these tears, could draw.

6

So the all-seeing sun each day
Distills the world with chemic ray,
But finds the essence only show'rs,
Which straight in pity back he pours.

7

Yet happy they whom grief doth bless,
That weep the more, and see the less:
And, to preserve their sight more true,
Bathe still their eyes in their own dew.

8

So Magdalen, in tears more wise
Dissolved those captivating eyes,
Whose liquid chains could flowing meet
To fetter her Redeemer's feet.

9

Not full sails hasting loaden home,
Nor the chaste lady's pregnant womb,
Nor Cynthia teeming shows so fair,
As two eyes swoll'n with weeping are.

10

The sparkling glance that shoots desire,
Drenched in these waves does lose its fire.
Yea, oft the Thunderer pity takes
And here the hissing lightning slakes.

11

The incense was to heaven dear,
Not as a perfume, but a tear.

And stars show lovely in the night,
But as they seem the tears of light.

12

Ope then, mine eyes, your double sluice,
And practise so your noblest use;
For others too can see, or sleep,
But only human eyes can weep.

13

Now, like two clouds dissolving, drop,
And at each tear in distance stop:
Now, like two fountains, trickle down;
Now, like two floods o'erturn and drown.

14

Thus let your streams o'erflow your springs,
Till eyes and tears be the same things:
And each the other's difference bears;
These weeping eyes, those seeing tears.

An Horatian Ode upon Cromwell's Return from Ireland

The forward youth that would appear
Must now forsake his muses dear,
   Nor in the shadows sing
   His numbers languishing.
'Tis time to leave the books in dust,
And oil the unusèd armour's rust:
   Removing from the wall
   The corslet of the hall.
So restless Cromwell could not cease
In the inglorious arts of peace,

But through adventurous war
    Urgèd his active star.
And, like the three-forked lightning, first
Breaking the clouds where it was nursed,
    Did thorough his own side
    His fiery way divide.
(For 'tis all one to courage high
The emulous or enemy:
    And with such to inclose
    Is more than to oppose.)
Then burning through the air he went,
And palaces and temples rent:
    And Caesar's head at last
    Did through his laurels blast.
'Tis madness to resist or blame
The force of angry heaven's flame:
    And, if we would speak true,
    Much to the man is due,
Who, from his private gardens, where
He lived reservèd and austere,
    As if his highest plot
    To plant the bergamot,
Could by industrious valour climb
To ruin the great work of time,
    And cast the kingdoms old
    Into another mould.
Though justice against fate complain,
And plead the ancient rights in vain:
    But those do hold or break
    As men are strong or weak.
Nature, that hateth emptiness,
Allows of penetration less:
    And therefore must make room
    Where greater spirits come.

What field of all the Civil Wars,
Where his were not the deepest scars?
    And Hampton shows what part
    He had of wiser art,
Where, twining subtle fears with hope,
He wove a net of such a scope,
    That Charles himself might chase
    To Carisbrooke's narrow case:
That thence the royal actor born
The tragic scaffold might adorn:
    While round the armèd bands
    Did clap their bloody hands.
He nothing common did or mean
Upon that memorable scene:
    But with his keener eye
    The axe's edge did try:
Nor called the gods with vulgar spite
To vindicate his helpless right,
    But bowed his comely head,
    Down, as upon a bed.
This was that memorable hour
Which first assured the forcèd power.
    So when they did design
    The Capitol's first line,
A bleeding head where they begun,
Did fright the architects to run;
    And yet in that the State
    Foresaw its happy fate.
And now the Irish are ashamed
To see themselves in one year tamed:
    So much one man can do,
    That does both act and know.
They can affirm his praises best,
And have, though overcome, confessed

How good he is, how just,
    And fit for highest trust:
Nor yet grown stiffer with command,
But still in the Republic's hand:
    How fit he is to sway
    That can so well obey.
He to the Commons' feet presents
A kingdom, for his first year's rents:
    And, what he may, forbears
    His fame, to make it theirs:
And has his sword and spoils ungirt,
To lay them at the public's skirt.
    So when the falcon high
    Falls heavy from the sky,
She, having killed, no more does search
But on the next green bough to perch,
    Where, when he first does lure,
    The falc'ner has her sure.
What may not then our isle presume
While Victory his crest does plume?
    What may not others fear
    If thus he crowns each year?
A Caesar, he, ere long to Gaul,
To Italy an Hannibal,
    And to all states not free
    Shall climactéric be.
The Pict no shelter now shall find
Within his parti-coloured mind,
    But from this valour sad
    Shrink underneath the plaid:
Happy, if in the tufted brake
The English hunter him mistake,
    Nor lay his hounds in near
    The Caledonian deer.

But thou, the Wars' and Fortune's son,
March indefatigably on,
    And for the last effect
    Still keep thy sword erect:
Besides the force it has to fright
The spirits of the shady night,
    The same arts that did gain
    A power, must it maintain.

Tom May's Death

As one put drunk into the packet-boat,
Tom May was hurried hence and did not know't.
But was amazed on the Elysian side,
And with an eye uncertain, gazing wide,
Could not determine in what place he was,
(For whence, in Stephen's Alley, trees or grass?)
Nor where The Pope's Head, nor The Mitre lay,
Signs by which still he found and lost his way.
At last while doubtfully he all compares,
He saw near hand, as he imagined, Ayres.
Such did he seem for corpulence and port,
But 'twas a man much of another sort;
'Twas Ben that in the dusky laurel shade
Amongst the chorus of old poets layed,
Sounding of ancient heroes, such as were
The subjects' safety, and the rebels' fear,
And how a double-headed vulture eats
Brutus and Cassius, the people's cheats.
But seeing May, he varied straight his song,
Gently to signify that he was wrong.
'Cups more than civil of Emathian wine,
I sing' (said he) 'and the Pharsalian Sign,

Where the historian of the commonwealth
In his own bowels sheathed the conquering health.'
By this, May to himself and them was come,
He found he was translated, and by whom,
Yet then with foot as stumbling as his tongue
Pressed for his place among the learned throng.
But Ben, who knew not neither foe nor friend,
Sworn enemy to all that do pretend,
Rose; more than ever he was seen severe,
Shook his gray locks, and his own bays did tear
At this intrusion. Then with laurel wand—
The awful sign of his supreme command,
At whose dread whisk Virgil himself does quake,
And Horace patiently its stroke does take—
As he crowds in, he whipped him o'er the pate
Like Pembroke at the masque, and then did rate:
  'Far from these blessed shades tread back again
Most servile wit, and mercenary pen,
Polydore, Lucan, Alan, Vandal, Goth,
Malignant poet and historian both,
Go seek the novice statesmen, and obtrude
On them some Roman-cast similitude,
Tell them of liberty, the stories fine,
Until you all grow consuls in your wine;
Or thou, Dictator of the glass, bestow
On him the Cato, this the Cicero,
Transferring old Rome hither in your talk,
As Bethlem's House did to Loreto walk.
Foul architect, that hadst not eye to see
How ill the measures of these states agree,
And who by Rome's example England lay,
Those but to Lucan do continue May.
But thee nor ignorance nor seeming good
Misled, but malice fixed and understood.

Because some one than thee more worthy wears
The sacred laurel, hence are all these tears?
Must therefore all the world be set on flame,
Because a gázette-writer missed his aim?
And for a tankard-bearing muse must we
As for the basket, Guelphs and Ghib'llines be?
When the sword glitters o'er the judge's head,
And fear has coward churchmen silencèd,
Then is the poet's time, 'tis then he draws,
And single fights forsaken virtue's cause.
He, when the wheel of empire whirleth back,
And though the world's disjointed axle crack,
Sings still of ancient rights and better times,
Seeks wretched good, arraigns successful crimes.
But thou, base man, first prostituted hast
Our spotless knowledge and the studies chaste,
Apostatizing from our arts and us,
To turn the chronicler to Spartacus.
Yet wast thou taken hence with equal fate,
Before thou couldst great Charles his death relate.
But what will deeper wound thy little mind,
Hast left surviving D'Avenant still behind,
Who laughs to see in this thy death renewed,
Right Roman poverty and gratitude.
Poor poet thou, and grateful senate they,
Who thy last reckoning did so largely pay,
And with the public gravity would come,
When thou hadst drunk thy last to lead thee home,
If that can be thy home where Spenser lies,
And reverend Chaucer, but their dust does rise
Against thee, and expels thee from their side,
As th' eagle's plumes from other birds divide.
Nor here thy shade must dwell. Return, return,
Where sulphury Phlegethon does ever burn.

Thee Cerberus with all his jaws shall gnash,
Megaera thee with all her serpents lash.
Thou riveted unto Ixion's wheel
Shalt break, and the perpetual vulture feel.
'Tis just, what torments poets e'er did feign,
Thou first historically shouldst sustain.'
    Thus, by irrevocable sentence cast,
May, only Master of these Revels, passed.
And straight he vanished in a cloud of pitch,
Such as unto the Sabbath bears the witch.

The Picture of Little T.C. in a Prospect of Flowers

1

See with what simplicity
This nymph begins her golden days!
In the green grass she loves to lie,
And there with her fair aspect tames
The wilder flowers, and gives them names:
But only with the roses plays;
        And them does tell
What colour best becomes them, and what smell.

2

Who can foretell for what high cause
This Darling of the Gods was born!
Yet this is she whose chaster laws
The wanton Love shall one day fear,
And, under her command severe,
See his bow broke and ensigns torn.
        Happy, who can
Appease this virtuous enemy of man!

3

O, then let me in time compound,
And parley with those conquering eyes;
Ere they have tried their force to wound,
Ere, with their glancing wheels, they drive
In triumph over hearts that strive,
And them that yield but more despise.
                Let me be laid,
Where I may see thy glories from some shade.

4

Meantime, whilst every verdant thing
Itself does at thy beauty charm,
Reform the errors of the spring;
Make that the tulips may have share
Of sweetness, seeing they are fair;
And roses of their thorns disarm:
                But most procure
That violets may a longer age endure.

5

But, O young beauty of the woods,
Whom Nature courts with fruits and flowers,
Gather the flowers, but spare the buds;
Lest Flora angry at thy crime,
To kill her infants in their prime,
Do quickly make the example yours;
                And, ere we see,
Nip in the blossom all our hopes and thee.

The Nymph Complaining for the Death of Her Fawn

The wanton troopers riding by
Have shot my fawn, and it will die.
Ungentle men! They cannot thrive—
To kill thee! Thou ne'er didst alive
Them any harm: alas, nor could
Thy death yet do them any good.
I'm sure I never wished them ill;
Nor do I for all this; nor will:
But if my simple prayers may yet
Prevail with heaven to forget
Thy murder, I will join my tears
Rather than fail. But, O my fears!
It cannot die so. Heaven's King
Keeps register of everything:
And nothing may we use in vain.
E'en beasts must be with justice slain,
Else men are made their deodands.
Though they should wash their guilty hands
In this warm life-blood, which doth part
From thine, and wound me to the heart,
Yet could they not be clean: their stain
Is dyed in such a purple grain,
There is not such another in
The world, to offer for their sin.

    Unconstant Sylvio, when yet
I had not found him counterfeit,
One morning (I remember well),
Tied in this silver chain and bell
Gave it to me: nay, and I know
What he said then; I'm sure I do.
Said he, 'Look how your huntsman here
Hath taught a fawn to hunt his *dear.*'

But Sylvio soon had me beguiled.
This waxèd tame, while he grew wild,
And quite regardless of my smart,
Left me his fawn, but took his heart.

    Thenceforth I set myself to play
My solitary time away
With this: and very well content,
Could so mine idle life have spent.
For it was full of sport; and light
Of foot, and heart; and did invite
Me to its game; it seemed to bless
Itself in me. How could I less
Than love it? O I cannot be
Unkind, t'a beast that loveth me.

    Had it lived long, I do not know
Whether it too might have done so
As Sylvio did: his gifts might be
Perhaps as false or more than he.
But I am sure, for ought that I
Could in so short a time espy,
Thy love was far more better than
The love of false and cruel men.

    With sweetest milk, and sugar, first
I it at mine own fingers nursed.
And as it grew, so every day
It waxed more white and sweet than they.
It had so sweet a breath! And oft
I blushed to see its foot more soft,
And white (shall I say than my hand?)
Nay, any lady's of the land.

    It is a wondrous thing, how fleet
'Twas on those little silver feet.
With what a pretty skipping grace,
It oft would challenge me the race:

And when 't had left me far away,
'Twould stay, and run again, and stay.
For it was nimbler much than hinds;
And trod, as on the foúr winds.
   I have a garden of my own
But so with roses overgrown,
And lilies, that you would it guess
To be a little wilderness.
And all the springtime of the year
It only lovèd to be there.
Among the beds of lilies, I
Have sought it oft, where it should lie;
Yet could not, till itself would rise,
Find it, although before mine eyes.
For, in the flaxen lilies' shade,
It like a bank of lilies laid.
Upon the roses it would feed,
Until its lips e'en seemed to bleed:
And then to me 'twould boldly trip,
And print those roses on my lip.
But all its chief delight was still
On roses thus itself to fill:
And its pure virgin limbs to fold
In whitest sheets of lilies cold.
Had it lived long, it would have been
Lilies without, roses within.
   O help! O help! I see it faint:
And die as calmly as a saint.
See how it weeps. The tears do come
Sad, slowly dropping like a gum.
So weeps the wounded balsam: so
The holy frankincense doth flow.
The brotherless Heliades
Melt in such amber tears as these.

I in a golden vial will
Keep these two crystal tears; and fill
It till it do o'erflow with mine;
Then place it in Diana's shrine.

Now my sweet fawn is vanished to
Whither the swans and turtles go:
In fair Elysium to endure,
With milk-white lambs, and ermines pure.
O do not run too fast: for I
Will but bespeak thy grave, and die.

First my unhappy statue shall
Be cut in marble; and withal,
Let it be weeping too—but there
The engraver sure his art may spare,
For I so truly thee bemoan,
That I shall weep though I be stone:
Until my tears (still dropping) wear
My breast, themselves engraving there.
There at my feet shalt thou be laid,
Of purest alabaster made:
For I would have thine image be
White as I can, though not as thee.

Upon the Hill and Grove at Bilbrough

TO THE LORD FAIRFAX

1

See how the archèd earth does here
Rise in a perfect hemisphere!
The stiffest compass could not strike
A line more circular and like;
Nor softest pencil draw a brow

So equal as this hill does bow.
It seems as for a model laid,
And that the world by it was made.

2

Here learn, ye mountains more unjust,
Which to abrupter greatness thrust,
That do with your hook-shouldered height
The earth deform and heaven fright,
For whose excrescence, ill-designed,
Nature must a new centre find,
Learn here those humble steps to tread,
Which to securer glory lead.

3

See what a soft access and wide
Lies open to its grassy side;
Nor with the rugged path deters
The feet of breathless travellers.
See then how courteous it ascends,
And all the way it rises bends;
Nor for itself the height does gain,
But only strives to raise the plain.

4

Yet thus it all the field commands,
And in unenvied greatness stands,
Discerning further than the cliff
Of heaven-daring Tenerife.
How glad the weary seamen haste
When they salute it from the mast!
By night the Northern Star their way
Directs, and this no less by day.

Upon its crest this mountain grave
A plump of agèd trees does wave.
No hostile hand durst ere invade
With impious steel the sacred shade.
For something always did appear
Of the great Master's terror there:
And men could hear his armour still
Rattling through all the grove and hill.

Fear of the Master, and respect
Of the great Nymph, did it protect,
Vera the Nymph that him inspired,
To whom he often here retired,
And on these oaks engraved her name;
Such wounds alone these woods became:
But ere he well the barks could part
'Twas writ already in their heart.

For they ('tis credible) have sense,
As we, of love and reverence,
And underneath the coarser rind
The genius of the house do bind.
Hence they successes seem to know,
And in their Lord's advancement grow;
But in no memory were seen,
As under this, so straight and green.

Yet now no further strive to shoot,
Contented if they fix their root.
Nor to the wind's uncertain gust,

Their prudent heads too far intrust.
Only sometimes a fluttering breeze
Discourses with the breathing trees,
Which in their modest whispers name
Those acts that swelled the cheek of fame.

9

'Much other groves', say they, 'than these
And other hills him once did please.
Through groves of pikes he thundered then,
And mountains raised of dying men.
For all the civic garlands due
To him, our branches are but few.
Nor are our trunks enow to bear
The trophies of one fertile year.'

10

'Tis true, ye trees, nor ever spoke
More certain oracles in oak.
But peace, (if you his favour prize):
That courage its own praises flies.
Therefore to your obscurer seats
From his own brightness he retreats:
Nor he the hills without the groves,
Nor height, but with retirement, loves.

Upon Appleton House

TO MY LORD FAIRFAX

1

Within this sober frame expect
Work of no foreign architect,

That unto caves the quarries drew,
And forests did to pastures hew,
Who of his great design in pain
Did for a model vault his brain,
Whose columns should so high be raised
To arch the brows that on them gazed.

2

Why should of all things man unruled
Such unproportioned dwellings build?
The beasts are by their dens expressed:
And birds contrive an equal nest;
The low-roofed tortoises do dwell
In cases fit of tortoise shell:
No creature loves an empty space;
Their bodies measure out their place.

3

But he, superfluously spread,
Demands more room alive than dead;
And in his hollow palace goes
Where winds (as he) themselves may lose;
What need of all this marble crust
T'impark the wanton mote of dust,
That thinks by breadth the world t'unite
Though the first builders failed in height?

4

But all things are composèd here
Like Nature, orderly and near:
In which we the dimensions find
Of that more sober age and mind,
When larger-sizèd men did stoop
To enter at a narrow loop;

As practising, in doors so strait,
To strain themselves through heaven's gate.

5

And surely when the after age
Shall hither come in pilgrimage,
These sacred places to adore,
By Vere and Fairfax trod before,
Men will dispute how their extent
Within such dwarfish confines went:
And some will smile at this, as well
As Romulus his bee-like cell.

6

Humility alone designs
Those short but admirable lines,
By which, ungirt and unconstrained,
Things greater are in less contained.
Let others vainly strive t'immure
The circle in the quadrature!
These holy mathematics can
In every figure equal man.

7

Yet thus the laden house does sweat,
And scarce endures the Master great:
But where he comes the swelling hall
Stirs, and the square grows spherical,
More by his magnitude distressed,
Then he is by its straitness pressed:
And too officiously it slights
That in itself which him delights.

8

So honour better lowness bears,
Than that unwonted greatness wears:
Height with a certain grace does bend,
But low things clownishly ascend.
And yet what needs there here excuse,
Where everything does answer use?
Where neatness nothing can condemn,
Nor pride invent what to contemn?

9

A stately frontispiece of poor
Adorns without the open door:
Nor less the rooms within commends
Daily new furniture of friends.
The house was built upon the place
Only as for a mark of grace;
And for an inn to entertain
Its Lord a while, but not remain.

10

Him Bishop's Hill or Denton may,
Or Bilbrough, better hold than they:
But Nature here hath been so free
As if she said, 'Leave this to me.'
Art would more neatly have defaced
What she had laid so sweetly waste,
In fragrant gardens, shady woods,
Deep meadows, and transparent floods.

11

While with slow eyes we these survey,
And on each pleasant footstep stay,
We opportunely may relate

The progress of this house's fate.
A nunnery first gave it birth
(For virgin buildings oft brought forth);
And all that neighbour-ruin shows
The quarries whence this dwelling rose.

12

Near to this gloomy cloister's gates
There dwelt the blooming virgin Thwaites,
Fair beyond measure, and an heir
Which might deformity make fair.
And oft she spent the summer suns
Discoursing with the subtle nuns.
Whence in these words one to her weaved,
(As 'twere by chance) thoughts long conceived.

13

'Within this holy leisure we
Live innocently, as you see.
These walls restrain the world without,
But hedge our liberty about.
These bars inclose that wider den
Of those wild creatures callèd men.
The cloister outward shuts its gates,
And, from us, locks on them the grates.

14

'Here we, in shining armour white,
Like virgin Amazons do fight.
And our chaste lamps we hourly trim,
Lest the great Bridegroom find them dim.
Our orient breaths perfumèd are
With incense of incessant prayer.

And holy-water of our tears
Most strangely our complexion clears.

15

'Not tears of grief; but such as those
With which calm pleasure overflows;
Or pity, when we look on you
That live without this happy vow.
How should we grieve that must be seen
Each one a spouse, and each a queen,
And can in heaven hence behold
Our brighter robes and crowns of gold?

16

'When we have prayèd all our beads,
Someone the holy legend reads;
While all the rest with needles paint
The face and graces of the saint.
But what the linen can't receive
They in their lives do interweave.
This work the saints best represents;
That serves for altar's ornaments.

17

'But much it to our work would add
If here your hand, your face we had:
By it we would Our Lady touch;
Yet thus She you resembles much.
Some of your features, as we sewed,
Through every shrine should be bestowed.
And in one beauty we would take
Enough a thousand saints to make.

'And (for I dare not quench the fire
That me does for your good inspire)
'Twere sacrilege a man t'admit
To holy things, for heaven fit.
I see the angels in a crown
On you the lilies showering down:
And around about you glory breaks,
That something more than human speaks.

'All beauty, when at such a height,
Is so already consecrate.
Fairfax I know; and long ere this
Have marked the youth, and what he is.
But can he such a rival seem
For whom you heav'n should disesteem?
Ah, no! and 'twould more honour prove
He your *devoto* were than love.

'Here live belovèd, and obeyed:
Each one your sister, each your maid.
And, if our rule seem strictly penned,
The rule itself to you shall bend.
Our abbess too, now far in age,
Doth your succession near presage.
How soft the yoke on us would lie,
Might such fair hands as yours it tie!

'Your voice, the sweetest of the choir,
Shall draw heaven nearer, raise us higher.
And your example, if our head,

Will soon us to perfection lead.
Those virtues to us all so dear,
Will straight grow sanctity when here:
And that, once sprung, increase so fast
Till miracles it work at last.

22

'Nor is our order yet so nice,
Delight to banish as a vice.
Here pleasure piety doth meet;
One pérfecting the other sweet.
So through the mortal fruit we boil
The sugar's uncorrupting oil:
And that which perished while we pull,
Is thus preservèd clear and full.

23

'For such indeed are all our arts,
Still handling Nature's finest parts.
Flowers dress the altars; for the clothes,
The sea-born amber we compose;
Balms for the grieved we draw; and pastes
We mold, as baits for curious tastes.
What need is here of man? unless
These as sweet sins we should confess.

24

'Each night among us to your side
Appoint a fresh and virgin bride;
Whom if Our Lord at midnight find,
Yet neither should be left behind.
Where you may lie as chaste in bed,
As pearls together billeted,

All night embracing arm in arm
Like crystal pure with cotton warm.

25

'But what is this to all the store
Of joys you see, and may make more!
Try but a while, if you be wise:
The trial neither costs, nor ties.'
Now, Fairfax, seek her promised faith:
Religion that dispensèd hath,
Which she henceforward does begin;
The nun's smooth tongue has sucked her in.

26

Oft, though he knew it was in vain,
Yet would he valiantly complain.
'Is this that sanctity so great,
An art by which you finelier cheat?
Hypocrite witches, hence avaunt,
Who though in prison yet enchant!
Death only can such thieves make fast,
As rob though in the dungeon cast.

27

'Were there but, when this house was made,
One stone that a just hand had laid,
It must have fall'n upon her head
Who first thee from thy faith misled.
And yet, how well soever meant,
With them 'twould soon grow fraudulent:
For like themselves they alter all,
And vice infects the very wall.

28

'But sure those buildings last not long,
Founded by folly, kept by wrong.
I know what fruit their gardens yield,
When they it think by night concealed.
Fly from their vices. 'Tis thy 'state,
Not thee, that they would consecrate.
Fly from their ruin. How I fear,
Though guiltless, lest thou perish there.'

What should he do? He would respect
Religion, but not right neglect:
For first religion taught him right,
And dazzled not but cleared his sight.
Sometimes resolved, his sword he draws,
But reverenceth then the laws:
For justice still that courage led;
First from a judge, then soldier bred.

Small honour would be in the storm.
The court him grants the lawful form;
Which licensed either peace or force,
To hinder the unjust divorce.
Yet still the nuns his right debarred,
Standing upon their holy guard.
Ill-counselled women, do you know
Whom you resist, or what you do?

Is not this he whose offspring fierce
Shall fight through all the universe;
And with successive valour try

France, Poland, either Germany;
Till one, as long since prophesied,
His horse through conquered Britain ride?
Yet, against fate, his spouse they kept,
And the great race would intercept.

32

Some to the breach against their foes
Their wooden saints in vain oppose.
Another bolder stands at push
With their old holy-water brush.
While the disjointed abbess threads
The jingling chain-shot of her beads.
But their loudest cannon were their lungs;
And sharpest weapons were their tongues.

33

But waving these aside like flies,
Young Fairfax through the wall does rise.
Then th' unfrequented vault appeared,
And superstitions vainly feared.
The relics false were set to view;
Only the jewels there were true—
But truly bright and holy Thwaites
That weeping at the altar waits.

34

But the glad youth away her bears,
And to the nuns bequeaths her tears:
Who guiltily their prize bemoan,
Like gypsies that a child had stolen.
Thenceforth (as when the enchantment ends,
The castle vanishes or rends)

The wasting cloister with the rest
Was in one instant dispossessed.

35

At the demolishing, this seat
To Fairfax fell as by escheat.
And what both nuns and founders willed
'Tis likely better thus fulfilled.
For if the virgin proved not theirs,
The cloister yet remainèd hers.
Though many a nun there made her vow,
'Twas no religious house till now.

36

From that blest bed the hero came,
Whom France and Poland yet does fame:
Who, when retirèd here to peace,
His warlike studies could not cease;
But laid these gardens out in sport
In the just figure of a fort;
And with five bastions it did fence,
As aiming one for every sense.

37

When in the east the morning ray
Hangs out the colours of the day,
The bee through these known alleys hums,
Beating the *dian* with its drums.
Then flowers their drowsy eyelids raise,
Their silken ensigns each displays,
And dries its pan yet dank with dew,
And fills its flask with odours new.

These, as their Governor goes by,
In fragrant volleys they let fly;
And to salute their Governess
Again as great a charge they press:
None for the virgin Nymph; for she
Seems with the flowers a flower to be.
And think so still! though not compare
With breath so sweet, or cheek so fair.

Well shot, ye firemen! Oh how sweet,
And round your equal fires do meet,
Whose shrill report no ear can tell,
But echoes to the eye and smell.
See how the flowers, as at parade,
Under their colours stand displayed:
Each regiment in order grows,
That of the tulip, pink, and rose.

But when the vigilant patrol
Of stars walks round about the Pole,
Their leaves, that to the stalks are curled,
Seem to their staves the ensigns furled.
Then in some flower's belovèd hut
Each bee as sentinel is shut,
And sleeps so too: but, if once stirred,
She runs you through, nor asks the word.

Oh thou, that dear and happy isle
The garden of the world ere while,
Thou paradise of foúr seas,

Which heaven planted us to please,
But, to exclude the world, did guard
With watery if not flaming sword;
What luckless apple did we taste,
To make us mortal, and thee waste?

42

Unhappy! shall we never more
That sweet militia restore,
When gardens only had their towers,
And all the garrisons were flowers,
When roses only arms might bear,
And men did rosy garlands wear?
Tulips, in several colours barred,
Were then the Switzers of our Guard.

43

The gardener had the soldier's place,
And his more gentle forts did trace.
The nursery of all things green
Was then the only magazine.
The winter quarters were the stoves,
Where he the tender plants removes.
But war all this doth overgrow;
We ordnance plant and powder sow.

44

And yet there walks one on the sod
Who, had it pleasèd him and God,
Might once have made our gardens spring
Fresh as his own and flourishing.
But he preferred to the Cinque Ports
These five imaginary forts,

And, in those half-dry trenches, spanned
Power which the ocean might command.

45

For he did, with his utmost skill,
Ambition weed, but conscience till—
Conscience, that heaven-nursèd plant,
Which most our earthy gardens want.
A prickling leaf it bears, and such
As that which shrinks at every touch;
But flowers eternal, and divine,
That in the crowns of saints do shine.

46

The sight does from these bastions ply,
The invisible artillery;
And at proud Cawood Castle seems
To point the battery of its beams.
As if it quarrelled in the seat
The ambition of its prelate great.
But o'er the meads below it plays,
Or innocently seems to graze.

47

And now to the abyss I pass
Of that unfathomable grass,
Where men like grasshoppers appear,
But grasshoppers are giants there:
They, in their squeaking laugh, contemn
Us as we walk more low than them:
And, from the precipices tall
Of the green spires, to us do call.

48

To see men through this meadow dive,
We wonder how they rise alive,
As, under water, none does know
Whether he fall through it or go.
But, as the mariners that sound,
And show upon their lead the ground,
They bring up flowers so to be seen,
And prove they've at the bottom been.

49

No scene that turns with engines strange
Does oftener than these meadows change.
For when the sun the grass hath vexed,
The tawny mowers enter next;
Who seem like Israelites to be,
Walking on foot through a green sea.
To them the grassy deeps divide,
And crowd a lane to either side.

50

With whistling scythe, and elbow strong,
These massacre the grass along:
While one, unknowing, carves the rail,
Whose yet unfeathered quills her fail.
The edge all bloody from its breast
He draws, and does his stroke detest,
Fearing the flesh untimely mowed
To him a fate as black forebode.

51

But bloody Thestylis, that waits
To bring the mowing camp their cates,
Greedy as kites, has trussed it up,

And forthwith means on it to sup:
When on another quick she lights,
And cries, 'He called us Israelites;
But now, to make his saying true,
Rails rain for quails, for manna, dew.'

52

Unhappy birds! what does it boot
To build below the grass's root;
When lowness is unsafe as height,
And chance o'ertakes, what 'scapeth spite?
And now your orphan parents' call
Sounds your untimely funeral.
Death-trumpets creak in such a note,
And 'tis the sourdine in their throat.

53

Or sooner hatch or higher build:
The mower now commands the field,
In whose new traverse seemeth wrought
A camp of battle newly fought:
Where, as the meads with hay, the plain
Lies quilted o'er with bodies slain:
The women that with forks it fling,
Do represent the pillaging.

54

And now the careless victors play,
Dancing the triumphs of the hay;
Where every mower's wholesome heat
Smells like an Alexander's sweat.
Their females fragrant as the mead
Which they in fairy circles tread:

When at their dance's end they kiss,
Their new-made hay not sweeter is.

55

When after this 'tis piled in cocks,
Like a calm sea it shows the rocks,
We wondering in the river near
How boats among them safely steer.
Or, like the desert Memphis sand,
Short pyramids of hay do stand.
And such the Roman camps do rise
In hills for soldiers' obsequies.

56

This scene again withdrawing brings
A new and empty face of things,
A levelled space, as smooth and plain
As cloths for Lely stretched to stain.
The world when first created sure
Was such a table rase and pure.
Or rather such is the *toril*
Ere the bulls enter at Madril.

57

For to this naked equal flat,
Which Levellers take pattern at,
The villagers in common chase
Their cattle, which it closer rase;
And what below the scythe increased
Is pinched yet nearer by the beast.
Such, in the painted world, appeared
D'Avenant with the universal herd.

They seem within the polished grass
A landskip drawn in looking-glass,
And shrunk in the huge pasture show
As spots, so shaped, on faces do—
Such fleas, ere they approach the eye,
In multiplying glasses lie.
They feed so wide, so slowly move,
As constellations do above.

Then, to conclude these pleasant acts,
Denton sets ope its cataracts,
And makes the meadow truly be
(What it but seemed before) a sea.
For, jealous of its Lord's long stay,
It tries t'invite him thus away.
The river in itself is drowned,
And isles the astonished cattle round.

Let others tell the paradox,
How eels now bellow in the ox;
How horses at their tails do kick,
Turned as they hang to leeches quick;
How boats can over bridges sail;
And fishes do the stables scale.
How salmons trespassing are found;
And pikes are taken in the pound.

But I, retiring from the flood,
Take sanctuary in the wood,
And, while it lasts, myself embark

In this yet green, yet growing ark,
Where the first carpenter might best
Fit timber for his keel have pressed.
And where all creatures might have shares,
Although in armies, not in pairs.

62

The double wood of ancient stocks,
Linked in so thick, an union locks,
It like two pedigrees appears,
On th' one hand Fairfax, th' other Vere's:
Of whom though many fell in war,
Yet more to heaven shooting are:
And, as they Nature's cradle decked,
Will in green age her hearse expect.

63

When first the eye this forest sees
It seems indeed as wood not trees:
As if their neighbourhood so old
To one great trunk them all did mould.
There the huge bulk takes place, as meant
To thrust up a fifth element,
And stretches still so closely wedged
As if the night within were hedged.

64

Dark all without it knits; within
It opens passable and thin;
And in as loose an order grows,
As the Corinthean porticoes.
The arching boughs unite between
The columns of the temple green;

And underneath the wingèd choirs
Echo about their tunèd fires.

65

The nightingale does here make choice
To sing the trials of her voice.
Low shrubs she sits in, and adorns
With music high the squatted thorns.
But highest oaks stoop down to hear,
And listening elders prick the ear.
The thorn, lest it should hurt her, draws
Within the skin its shrunken claws.

66

But I have for my music found
A sadder, yet more pleasing sound:
The stock-doves, whose fair necks are graced
With nuptial rings, their ensigns chaste;
Yet always, for some cause unknown,
Sad pair unto the elms they moan.
O why should such a couple mourn,
That in so equal flames do burn!

67

Then as I careless on the bed
Of gelid strawberries do tread,
And through the hazels thick espy
The hatching throstles shining eye,
The heron from the ash's top,
The eldest of its young lets drop,
As if it stork-like did pretend
That tribute to its Lord to send.

But most the hewel's wonders are,
Who here has the holtfelster's care.
He walks still upright from the root,
Measuring the timber with his foot,
And all the way, to keep it clean,
Doth from the bark the woodmoths glean.
He, with his beak, examines well
Which fit to stand and which to fell.

The good he numbers up, and hacks,
As if he marked them with the axe.
But where he, tinkling with his beak,
Does find the hollow oak to speak,
That for his building he designs,
And through the tainted side he mines.
Who could have thought the tallest oak
Should fall by such a feeble stroke!

Nor would it, had the tree not fed
A traitor-worm, within it bred,
(As first our flesh corrupt within
Tempts impotent and bashful sin).
And yet that worm triumphs not long,
But serves to feed the hewel's young,
While the oak seems to fall content,
Viewing the treason's punishment.

Thus I, easy philosopher,
Among the birds and trees confer.
And little now to make me wants

Or of the fowls, or of the plants:
Give me but wings as they, and I
Straight floating on the air shall fly:
Or turn me but, and you shall see
I was but an inverted tree.

72

Already I begin to call
In their most learn'd original:
And where I language want, my signs
The bird upon the bough divines;
And more attentive there doth sit
Than if she were with lime-twigs knit.
No leaf does tremble in the wind
Which I, returning, cannot find.

73

Out of these scattered sibyl's leaves
Strange prophecies my fancy weaves:
And in one history consumes,
Like Mexique paintings, all the plumes.
What Rome, Greece, Palestine, ere said
I in this light mosaic read.
Thrice happy he who, not mistook,
Hath read in Nature's mystic book.

74

And see how chance's better wit
Could with a mask my studies hit!
The oak leaves me embroider all,
Between which caterpillars crawl:
And ivy, with familiar trails,
Me licks, and clasps, and curls, and hales.

Under this antic cope I move
Like some great prelate of the grove.

75

Then, languishing with ease, I toss
On pallets swoll'n of velvet moss,
While the wind, cooling through the boughs,
Flatters with air my panting brows.
Thanks for my rest, ye mossy banks;
And unto you, cool zephyrs, thanks,
Who, as my hair, my thoughts too shed,
And winnow from the chaff my head.

76

How safe, methinks, and strong, behind
These trees have I encamped my mind:
Where beauty, aiming at the heart,
Bends in some tree its useless dart;
And where the world no certain shot
Can make, or me it toucheth not.
But I on it securely play,
And gall its horsemen all the day.

77

Bind me, ye woodbines, in your twines,
Curl me about, ye gadding vines,
And, oh, so close your circles lace,
That I may never leave this place:
But lest your fetters prove too weak,
Ere I your silken bondage break,
Do you, O brambles, chain me too,
And, courteous briars, nail me through.

Here in the morning tie my chain,
Where the two woods have made a lane,
While, like a guard on either side,
The trees before their Lord divide;
This, like a long and equal thread,
Betwixt two labyrinths does lead.
But where the floods did lately drown,
There at the evening stake me down.

For now the waves are fall'n and dried,
And now the meadows fresher dyed,
Whose grass, with moister colour dashed,
Seems as green silks but newly washed.
No serpent new nor crocodile
Remains behind our little Nile,
Unless itself you will mistake,
Among these meads the only snake.

See in what wanton harmless folds
It everywhere the meadow holds;
And its yet muddy back doth lick,
Till as a crystal mirror slick,
Where all things gaze themselves, and doubt
If they be in it or without.
And for his shade which therein shines,
Narcissus-like, the sun too pines.

Oh what a pleasure 'tis to hedge
My temples here with heavy sedge,
Abandoning my lazy side,

Stretched as a bank unto the tide,
Or to suspend my sliding foot
On th' osier's underminèd root,
And in its branches tough to hang,
While at my lines the fishes twang!

82

But now away my hooks, my quills,
And angles—idle utensils.
The young Maria walks tonight:
Hide, trifling youth, thy pleasures slight.
'Twere shame that such judicious eyes
Should with such toys a man surprise;
She, that already is the law
Of all her sex, her age's awe.

83

See how loose Nature, in respect
To her, itself doth recollect;
And everything so whisht and fine,
Starts forthwith to its *bonne mine.*
The sun himself, of her aware,
Seems to descend with greater care;
And lest she see him go to bed,
In blushing clouds conceals his head.

84

So when the shadows laid asleep
From underneath these banks do creep,
And on the river as it flows
With eben shuts begin to close;
The modest halcyon comes in sight,
Flying betwixt the day and night;

And such an horror calm and dumb,
Admiring Nature does benumb.

85

The viscous air, where'e'er she fly,
Follows and sucks her azure dye;
The jellying stream compacts below,
If it might fix her shadow so;
The stupid fishes hang, as plain
As flies in crystal overta'en;
And men the silent scene assist,
Charmed with the sapphire-wingèd mist.

86

Maria such, and so doth hush
The world, and through the evening rush.
No new-born comet such a train
Draws through the sky, nor star new-slain.
For straight those giddy rockets fail,
Which from the putrid earth exhale,
But by her flames, in heaven tried,
Nature is wholly vitrified.

87

'Tis she that to these gardens gave
That wondrous beauty which they have;
She straightness on the woods bestows;
To her the meadow sweetness owes;
Nothing could make the river be
So crystal pure but only she;
She yet more pure, sweet, straight, and fair,
Than gardens, woods, meads, rivers are.

Therefore what first she on them spent,
They gratefully again present:
The meadow, carpets where to tread;
The garden, flow'rs to crown her head;
And for a glass, the limpid brook,
Where she may all her beauties look;
But, since she would not have them seen,
The wood about her draws a screen.

89

For she, to higher beauties raised,
Disdains to be for lesser praised.
She counts her beauty to converse
In all the languages as hers;
Nor yet in those herself employs
But for the wisdom, not the noise;
Nor yet that wisdom would affect,
But as 'tis heaven's dialect.

90

Blest Nymph! that couldst so soon prevent
Those trains by youth against thee meant:
Tears (watery shot that pierce the mind);
And signs (Love's cannon charged with wind);
True praise (that breaks through all defence);
And feigned complying innocence;
But knowing where this ambush lay,
She 'scaped the safe, but roughest way.

91

This 'tis to have been from the first
In a domestic heaven nursed,
Under the discipline severe

Of Fairfax, and the starry Vere;
Where not one object can come nigh
But pure, and spotless as the eye;
And goodness doth itself entail
On females, if there want a male.

92

Go now, fond sex, that on your face
Do all your useless study place,
Nor once at vice your brows dare knit
Lest the smooth forehead wrinkled sit:
Yet your own face shall at you grin,
Thorough the black-bag of your skin,
When knowledge only could have filled
And virtue all those furrows tilled.

93

Hence she with graces more divine
Supplies beyond her sex the line;
And like a sprig of mistletoe
On the Fairfacian oak does grow;
Whence, for some universal good,
The priest shall cut the sacred bud,
While her glad parents most rejoice,
And make their destiny their choice.

94

Meantime, ye fields, springs, bushes, flowers,
Where yet she leads her studious hours,
(Till fate her worthily translates,
And find a Fairfax for our Thwaites),
Employ the means you have by her,
And in your kind yourselves prefer;

That, as all virgins she precedes,
So you all woods, streams, gardens, meads.

95

For you, Thessalian Tempe's seat
Shall now be scorned as obsolete;
Aranjuez, as less, disdained;
The Bel-Retiro as constrained;
But name not the Idalian grove—
For 'twas the seat of wanton love—
Much less the dead's Elysian Fields,
Yet nor to them your beauty yields.

96

'Tis not, what once it was, the world,
But a rude heap together hurled,
All negligently overthrown,
Gulfs, deserts, precipices, stone.
Your lesser world contains the same,
But in more decent order tame;
You, heaven's centre, Nature's lap,
And paradise's only map.

97

But now the salmon-fishers moist
Their leathern boats begin to hoist,
And like Antipodes in shoes,
Have shod their heads in their canoes.
How tortoise-like, but not so slow,
These rational amphibii go!
Let's in: for the dark hemisphere
Does now like one of them appear.

The Garden

1

How vainly men themselves amaze
To win the palm, the oak, or bays,
And their uncessant labours see
Crowned from some single herb or tree,
Whose short and narrow vergèd shade
Does prudently their toils upbraid,
While all flow'rs and all trees do close
To weave the garlands of repose.

2

Fair Quiet, have I found thee here,
And Innocence, thy sister dear!
Mistaken long, I sought you then
In busy companies of men.
Your sacred plants, if here below,
Only among the plants will grow.
Society is all but rude,
To this delicious solitude.

3

No white nor red was ever seen
So am'rous as this lovely green.
Fond lovers, cruel as their flame,
Cut in these trees their mistress' name.
Little, alas, they know, or heed,
How far these beauties hers exceed!
Fair trees! wheres'e'er your barks I wound,
No name shall but your own be found.

4

When we have run our passion's heat,
Love hither makes his best retreat.
The gods, that mortal beauty chase,
Still in a tree did end their race.
Apollo hunted Daphne so,
Only that she might laurel grow.
And Pan did after Syrinx speed,
Not as a nymph, but for a reed.

5

What wondrous life is this I lead!
Ripe apples drop about my head;
The luscious clusters of the vine
Upon my mouth do crush their wine;
The nectarene, and curious peach,
Into my hands themselves do reach;
Stumbling on melons, as I pass,
Ensnared with flowers, I fall on grass.

6

Meanwhile the mind, from pleasures less,
Withdraws into its happiness:
The mind, that ocean where each kind
Does straight its own resemblance find,
Yet it creates, transcending these,
Far other worlds, and other seas,
Annihilating all that's made
To a green thought in a green shade.

7

Here at the fountain's sliding foot,
Or at some fruit-tree's mossy root,
Casting the body's vest aside,

My soul into the boughs does glide:
There like a bird it sits, and sings,
Then whets, and combs its silver wings;
And, till prepared for longer flight,
Waves in its plumes the various light.

8

Such was that happy garden-state,
While man there walked without a mate:
After a place so pure, and sweet,
What other help could yet be meet!
But 'twas beyond a mortal's share
To wander solitary there:
Two paradises 'twere in one
To live in paradise alone.

9

How well the skilful gardener drew
Of flowers and herbs this dial new,
Where from above the milder sun
Does through a fragrant zodiac run;
And, as it works, the industrious bee
Computes its time as well as we.
How could such sweet and wholesome hours
Be reckoned but with herbs and flowers!

On a Drop of Dew

See how the orient dew,
Shed from the bosom of the morn
    Into the blowing roses,
Yet careless of its mansion new,
For the clear region where 'twas born

Round in itself incloses:
And in its little globe's extent,
Frames as it can its native element.
How it the purple flow'r does slight,
Scarce touching where it lies,
But gazing back upon the skies,
Shines with a mournful light,
Like its own tear,
Because so long divided from the sphere.
Restless it rolls and unsecure,
Trembling lest it grow impure,
Till the warm sun pity its pain,
And to the skies exhale it back again.
So the soul, that drop, that ray
Of the clear fountain of eternal day,
Could it within the human flow'r be seen,
Remembering still its former height,
Shuns the sweet leaves and blossoms green,
And recollecting its own light,
Does, in its pure and circling thoughts, express
The greater heaven in an heaven less.
In how coy a figure wound,
Every way it turns away:
So the world excluding round,
Yet receiving in the day,
Dark beneath, but bright above,
Here disdaining, there in love.
How loose and easy hence to go,
How girt and ready to ascend,
Moving but on a point below,
It all about does upwards bend.
Such did the manna's sacred dew distill,
White and entire, though congealed and chill,

Congealed on earth: but does, dissolving, run
Into the glories of th' almighty sun.

A Dialogue between the Soul and Body

SOUL

O, who shall from this dungeon raise
A soul, enslaved so many ways,
With bolts of bones, that fettered stands
In feet, and manacled in hands.
Here blinded with an eye; and there
Deaf with the drumming of an ear,
A soul hung up, as 'twere, in chains
Of nerves, and arteries, and veins,
Tortured, besides each other part,
In a vain head, and double heart?

BODY

O, who shall me deliver whole,
From bonds of this tyrannic soul,
Which, stretched upright, impales me so,
That mine own precipice I go;
And warms and moves this needless frame
(A fever could but do the same),
And, wanting where its spite to try,
Has made me live to let me die,
A body that could never rest,
Since this ill spirit it possessed?

SOUL

What magic could me thus confine
Within another's grief to pine,
Where, whatsoever it complain,
I feel, that cannot feel, the pain,

And all my care itself employs,
That to preserve, which me destroys:
Constrained not only to endure
Diseases, but, what's worse, the cure:
And ready oft the port to gain,
Am shipwrecked into health again?

BODY

But physic yet could never reach
The maladies thou me dost teach:
Whom first the cramp of hope does tear,
And then the palsy shakes of fear;
The pestilence of love does heat,
Or hatred's hidden ulcer eat;
Joy's cheerful madness does perplex,
Or sorrow's other madness vex;
Which knowledge forces me to know,
And memory will not forgo.
What but a soul could have the wit
To build me up for sin so fit?
So architects do square and hew,
Green trees that in the forest grew.

The Mower against Gardens

Luxurious man, to bring his vice in use,
    Did after him the world seduce,
And from the fields the flowers and plants allure,
    Where nature was most plain and pure.
He first enclosed within the gardens square
    A dead and standing pool of air,
And a more luscious earth for them did knead,
    Which stupified them while it fed.

The pink grew then as double as his mind;
   The nutriment did change the kind.
With strange perfumes he did the roses taint,
   And flowers themselves were taught to paint.
The tulip, white, did for complexion seek,
   And learned to interline its cheek:
Its onion root they then so high did hold,
   That one was for a meadow sold.
Another world was searched, through oceans new,
   To find the *Marvel of Peru*.
And yet these rarities might be allowed
   To man, that sovereign thing and proud,
Had he not dealt between the bark and tree,
   Forbidden mixtures there to see.
No plant now knew the stock from which it came;
   He grafts upon the wild the tame:
That th' uncertain and adulterate fruit
   Might put the palate in dispute.
His green seraglio has its eunuchs too,
   Lest any tyrant him outdo.
And in the cherry he does nature vex,
   To procreate without a sex.
'Tis all enforced, the fountain and the grot,
   While the sweet fields do lie forgot:
Where willing nature does to all dispense
   A wild and fragrant innocence:
And fauns and fairies do the meadows till,
   More by their presence than their skill.
Their statues, polished by some ancient hand,
   May to adorn the gardens stand:
But howsoe'er the figures do excel,
   The gods themselves with us do dwell.

Damon the Mower

1

Hark how the Mower Damon sung,
With love of Juliana stung!
While everything did seem to paint
The scene more fit for his complaint.
Like her fair eyes the day was fair,
But scorching like his am'rous care.
Sharp like his scythe his sorrow was,
And withered like his hopes the grass.

2

'Oh what unusual heats are here,
Which thus our sunburned meadows sear!
The grasshopper its pipe gives o'er;
And hamstringed frogs can dance no more.
But in the brook the green frog wades;
And grasshoppers seek out the shades.
Only the snake, that kept within,
Now glitters in its second skin.

3

'This heat the sun could never raise,
Nor Dog Star so inflame the days.
It from an higher beauty grow'th,
Which burns the fields and mower both:
Which mads the dog, and makes the sun
Hotter than his own Phaëton.
Not July causeth these extremes,
But Juliana's scorching beams.

4

'Tell me where I may pass the fires
Of the hot day, or hot desires.
To what cool cave shall I descend,
Or to what gelid fountain bend?
Alas! I look for ease in vain,
When remedies themselves complain.
No moisture but my tears do rest,
Nor cold but in her icy breast.

5

'How long wilt thou, fair shepherdess,
Esteem me, and my presents less?
To thee the harmless snake I bring,
Disarmèd of its teeth and sting;
To thee chameleons, changing hue,
And oak leaves tipped with honey dew.
Yet thou, ungrateful, hast not sought
Nor what they are, nor who them brought.

6

'I am the Mower Damon, known
Through all the meadows I have mown.
On me the morn her dew distills
Before her darling daffodils.
And, if at noon my toil me heat,
The sun himself licks off my sweat.
While, going home, the evening sweet
In cowslip-water bathes my feet.

7

'What, though the piping shepherd stock
The plains with an unnumbered flock,
This scythe of mine discovers wide

More ground than all his sheep do hide.
With this the golden fleece I shear
Of all these closes every year.
And though in wool more poor than they,
Yet am I richer far in hay.

8

'Nor am I so deformed to sight,
If in my scythe I lookèd right;
In which I see my picture done,
As in a crescent moon the sun.
The deathless fairies take me oft
To lead them in their dances soft:
And, when I tune myself to sing,
About me they contract their ring.

9

'How happy might I still have mowed,
Had not Love here his thistles sowed!
But now I all the day complain,
Joining my labour to my pain;
And with my scythe cut down the grass,
Yet still my grief is where it was:
But, when the iron blunter grows,
Sighing, I whet my scythe and woes.'

10

While thus he threw his elbow round,
Depopulating all the ground,
And, with his whistling scythe, does cut
Each stroke between the earth and root,
The edgèd steel by careless chance
Did into his own ankle glance;

And there among the grass fell down,
By his own scythe, the Mower mown.

11

'Alas!' said he, 'these hurts are slight
To those that die by love's despite.
With shepherd's-purse, and clown's-all-heal,
The blood I staunch, and wound I seal.
Only for him no cure is found,
Whom Juliana's eyes do wound.
'Tis death alone that this must do:
For Death thou art a Mower too.'

The Mower to the Glowworms

1

Ye living lamps, by whose dear light
The nightingale does sit so late,
And studying all the summer night,
Her matchless songs does meditate;

2

Ye country comets, that portend
No war, nor prince's funeral,
Shining unto no higher end
Than to presage the grass's fall;

3

Ye glowworms, whose officious flame
To wandering mowers shows the way,
That in the night have lost their aim,
And after foolish fires do stray;

Your courteous lights in vain you waste,
Since Juliana here is come,
For she my mind hath so displaced
That I shall never find my home.

The Mower's Song

1

My mind was once the true survey
Of all these meadows fresh and gay,
And in the greenness of the grass
Did see its hopes as in a glass;
When Juliana came, and she
What I do to the grass, does to my thoughts and me.

2

But these, while I with sorrow pine,
Grew more luxuriant still and fine,
That not one blade of grass you spied,
But had a flower on either side;
When Juliana came, and she
What I do to the grass, does to my thoughts and me.

3

Unthankful meadows, could you so
A fellowship so true forgo,
And in your gaudy May-games meet,
While I lay trodden under feet?
When Juliana came, and she
What I do to the grass, does to my thoughts and me.

But what you in compassion ought,
Shall now by my revenge be wrought:
And flow'rs, and grass, and I and all,
Will in one common ruin fall.
For Juliana comes, and she
What I do to the grass, does to my thoughts and me.

And thus, ye meadows, which have been
Companions of my thoughts more green,
Shall now the heraldry become
With which I will adorn my tomb;
For Juliana comes, and she
What I do to the grass, does to my thoughts and me.

Bermudas

Where the remote Bermudas ride
In the ocean's bosom unespied,
From a small boat, that rowed along,
The listening winds received this song.
  'What should we do but sing his praise
That led us through the watery maze,
Unto an isle so long unknown,
And yet far kinder than our own?
Where he the huge sea-monsters wracks,
That lift the deep upon their backs,
He lands us on a grassy stage,
Safe from the storms, and prelate's rage.
He gave us this eternal spring,
Which here enamels everything,
And sends the fowl to us in care,

On daily visits through the air.
He hangs in shades the orange bright,
Like golden lamps in a green night,
And does in the pom'granates close
Jewels more rich than Ormus shows.
He makes the figs our mouths to meet,
And throws the melons at our feet,
But apples plants of such a price,
No tree could ever bear them twice.
With cedars, chosen by his hand,
From Lebanon, he stores the land,
And makes the hollow seas, that roar,
Proclaim the ambergris on shore.
He cast (of which we rather boast)
The gospel's pearl upon our coast,
And in these rocks for us did frame
A temple, where to sound his name.
Oh let our voice his praise exalt,
Till it arrive at heaven's vault:
Which thence (perhaps) rebounding, may
Echo beyond the Mexique Bay.'
　　Thus sung they, in the English boat,
An holy and a cheerful note,
And all the way, to guide their chime,
With falling oars they kept the time.

A Poem upon the Death of His Late Highness the Lord Protector

That Providence which had so long the care
Of Cromwell's head, and numbered every hair,
Now in itself (the glass where all appears)
Had seen the period of his golden years:

And thenceforth only did attend to trace
What death might least so fair a life deface.

    The people, which what most they fear esteem,
Death when more horrid, so more noble deem,
And blame the last act, like spectators vain,
Unless the prince whom they applaud be slain.
Nor fate indeed can well refuse that right
To those that lived in war, to die in fight.

    But long his valour none had left that could
Endanger him, or clemency that would.
And he whom Nature all for peace had made,
But angry heaven unto war had swayed,
And so less useful where he most desired,
For what he least affected was admired,
Deservèd yet an end whose every part,
Should speak the wondrous softness of his heart.

    To Love and Grief the fatal writ was 'signed;
(Those nobler weaknesses of human kind,
From which those powers that issued the decree,
Although immortal, found they were not free),
That they, to whom his breast still open lies,
In gentle passions should his death disguise:
And leave succeeding ages cause to mourn,
As long as Grief shall weep, or Love shall burn.

    Straight does a slow and languishing disease
Eliza, Nature's and his darling, seize.
Her when an infant, taken with her charms,
He oft would flourish in his mighty arms,
And, lest their force the tender burden wrong,
Slacken the vigour of his muscles strong;
Then to the Mother's breast her softly move,
Which while she drained of milk, she filled with love.
But as with riper years her virtue grew,
And every minute adds a lustre new,

When with meridian height her beauty shined,
And thorough that sparkled her fairer mind,
When she with smiles serene in words discreet
His hidden soul at every turn could meet;
Then might y'ha' daily his affection spied,
Doubling that knot which destiny had tied,
While they by sense, not knowing, comprehend
How on each other both their fates depend.
With her each day the pleasing hours he shares,
And at her aspect calms his growing cares;
Or with a grandsire's joy her children sees
Hanging about her neck or at his knees.
Hold fast, dear infants, hold them both or none;
This will not stay when once the other's gone.

A silent fire now wastes those limbs of wax,
And him within his tortured image racks.
So the flower withering which the garden crowned,
The sad root pines in secret under ground.
Each groan he doubled and each sigh he sighed,
Repeated over to the restless night.
No trembling string composed to numbers new,
Answers the touch in notes more sad, more true.
She, lest he grieve, hides what she can her pains,
And he to lessen hers his sorrow feigns:
Yet both perceived, yet both concealed their skills,
And so diminishing increased their ills:
That whether by each other's grief they fell,
Or on their own redoubled, none can tell.

And now Eliza's purple locks were shorn,
Where she so long her Father's fate had worn:
And frequent lightning to her soul that flies,
Divides the air, and opens all the skies:
And now his life, suspended by her breath,
Ran out impetuously to hasting death.

Like polished mirrors, so his steely breast
Had every figure of her woes expressed,
And with the damp of her last gasp obscured,
Had drawn such stains as were not to be cured.
Fate could not either reach with single stroke,
But the dear image fled, the mirror broke.

Who now shall tell us more of mournful swans,
Of halcyons kind, or bleeding pelicans?
No downy breast did e'er so gently beat,
Or fan with airy plumes so soft an heat.
For he no duty by his height excused,
Nor, though a prince, to be a man refused:
But rather than in his Eliza's pain
Not love, not grieve, would neither live nor reign:
And in himself so oft immortal tried,
Yet in compassion of another died.

So have I seen a vine, whose lasting age
Of many a winter hath survived the rage,
Under whose shady tent men every year
At its rich blood's expense their sorrow cheer,
If some dear branch where it extends its life
Chance to be pruned by an untimely knife,
The parent-tree unto the grief succeeds,
And through the wound its vital humour bleeds,
Trickling in watery drops, whose flowing shape
Weeps that it falls ere fixed into a grape.
So the dry stock, no more that spreading vine,
Frustrates the autumn and the hopes of wine.

A secret cause does sure those signs ordain
Foreboding princes' falls, and seldom vain.
Whether some kinder powers that wish us well,
What they above cannot prevent foretell;
Or the great world do by consent presage,
As hollow seas with future tempests rage;

Or rather heaven, which us so long foresees,
Their funerals celebrates while it decrees.
But never yet was any human fate
By Nature solemnized with so much state.
He unconcerned the dreadful passage crossed;
But, oh, what pangs that death did Nature cost!
    First the great thunder was shot off, and sent
The signal from the starry battlement.
The winds receive it, and its force outdo,
As practising how they could thunder too;
Out of the binder's hand the sheaves they tore,
And thrashed the harvest in the airy floor;
Or of huge trees, whose growth with his did rise,
The deep foundations opened to the skies.
Then heavy show'rs the wingèd tempests lead,
And pour the deluge o'er the chaos' head.
The race of warlike horses at his tomb
Offer themselves in many a hecatomb;
With pensive head towards the ground they fall,
And helpless languish at the tainted stall.
Numbers of men decrease with pains unknown,
And hasten, not to see his death, their own.
Such tortures all the elements unfixed,
Troubled to part where so exactly mixed.
And as through air his wasting spirits flowed,
The universe laboured beneath their load.
    Nature, it seemed with him would Nature vie;
He with Eliza. It with him would die,
    He without noise still travelled to his end,
As silent suns to meet the night descend.
The stars that for him fought had only power
Left to determine now his fatal hour,
Which, since they might not hinder, yet they cast
To choose it worthy of his glories past.

No part of time but bare his mark away
Of honour; all the year was Cromwell's day:
But this, of all the most auspicious found,
Twice had in open field him victor crowned:
When up the armèd mountains of Dunbar
He marched, and through deep Severn ending war.
What day should him eternize but the same
That had before immortalized his name?
That so who ere would at his death have joyed,
In their own griefs might find themselves employed;
But those that sadly his departure grieved,
Yet joyed, remembering what he once achieved.
And the last minute his victorious ghost
Gave chase to Ligny on the Belgic coast.
Here ended all his mortal toils: he laid
And slept in peace under the laurel shade.

O Cromwell, Heaven's Favourite! To none
Have such high honours from above been shown:
For whom the elements we mourners see,
And heaven itself would the great herald be,
Which with more care set forth his obsequies
Than those of Moses hid from human eyes,
As jealous only here lest all be less,
That we could to his memory express.

Then let us to our course of mourning keep:
Where heaven leads, 'tis piety to weep.
Stand back, ye seas, and shrunk beneath the veil
Of your abyss, with covered head bewail
Your Monarch: we demand not your supplies
To compass in our isle; our tears suffice:
Since him away the dismal tempest rent,
Who once more joined us to the continent;
Who planted England on the Flandric shore,
And stretched our frontier to the Indian ore;

Whose greater truths obscure the fables old,
Whether of British saints or Worthies told;
And in a valour lessening Arthur's deeds,
For holiness the Confessor exceeds.

He first put arms into Religion's hand,
And timorous Conscience unto Courage manned:
The soldier taught that inward mail to wear,
And fearing God how they should nothing fear.
'Those strokes', he said, 'will pierce through all below
Where those that strike from heaven fetch their blow.'
Astonished armies did their flight prepare,
And cities strong were stormèd by his prayer;
Of that, forever Preston's field shall tell
The story, and impregnable Clonmel.
And where the sandy mountain Fenwick scaled,
The sea between, yet hence his prayer prevailed.
What man was ever so in heaven obeyed
Since the commanded sun o'er Gibeon stayed?
In all his wars needs must he triumph when
He conquered God still ere he fought with men:

Hence, though in battle none so brave or fierce,
Yet him the adverse steel could never pierce.
Pity it seemed to hurt him more that felt
Each wound himself which he to others dealt;
Danger itself refusing to offend
So loose an enemy, so fast a friend.

Friendship, that sacred virtue, long does claim
The first foundation of his house and name:
But within one its narrow limits fall,
His tenderness extended unto all.
And that deep soul through every channel flows,
Where kindly nature loves itself to lose.
More strong affections never reason served,
Yet still affected most what best deserved.

If he Eliza loved to that degree,
(Though who more worthy to be loved than she?)
If so indulgent to his own, how dear
To him the children of the highest were?
For her he once did nature's tribute pay:
For these his life adventured every day:
And 'twould be found, could we his thoughts have cast,
Their griefs struck deepest, if Eliza's last.

What prudence more than human did he need
To keep so dear, so differing minds agreed?
The worser sort, as conscious of their ill,
Lie weak and easy to the ruler's will;
But to the good (too many or too few)
All law is useless, all reward is due.
Oh ill-advised, if not for love, for shame,
Spare yet your own, if you neglect his fame;
Lest others dare to think your zeal a mask,
And you to govern, only *heaven's* task.

Valour, religion, friendship, prudence died
At once with him, and all that's good beside;
And we death's refuse, nature's dregs, confined
To loathsome life, alas! are left behind.
Where we (so once we used) shall now no more
To fetch day, press about his chamber door—
From which he issued with that awful state,
It seemed Mars broke through Janus' double gate,
Yet always tempered with an air so mild,
No April suns that e'er so gently smiled—
No more shall hear that powerful language charm,
Whose force oft spared the labour of his arm:
No more shall follow where he spent the days
In war, in counsel, or in prayer and praise,
Whose meanest acts he would himself advance,
As ungirt David to the ark did dance.

All, all is gone of ours or his delight
In horses fierce, wild deer, or armour bright;
Francisca fair can nothing now but weep,
Nor with soft notes shall sing his cares asleep.
   I saw him dead. A leaden slumber lies
And mortal sleep over those wakeful eyes:
Those gentle rays under the lids were fled,
Which through his looks that piercing sweetness shed;
That port which so majestic was and strong,
Loose and deprived of vigour, stretched along:
All withered, all discoloured, pale and wan—
How much another thing, nor more that man?
Of human glory vain, oh death, oh wings,
Oh worthless world, oh transitory things!
   Yet dwelt that greatness in his shape decayed,
That still though dead, greater than death he laid;
And in his altered face you something feign
That threatens death he yet will live again.
   Not much unlike the sacred oak which shoots
To heaven its branches and through earth its roots,
Whose spacious boughs are hung with trophies round,
And honoured wreaths have oft the victor crowned.
When angry Jove darts lightning through the air,
At mortals' sins, nor his own plant will spare,
(It groans, and bruises all below, that stood
So many years the shelter of the wood.)
The tree erewhile foreshortened to our view,
When fall'n shows taller yet than as it grew:
   So shall his praise to after times increase,
When truth shall be allowed, and faction cease,
And his own shadows with him fall. The eye
Detracts from objects than itself more high:
But when death takes them from that envied seat,
Seeing how little, we confess how great.

Thee, many ages hence in martial verse
Shall the English soldier, ere he charge, rehearse,
Singing of thee, inflame themselves to fight,
And with the name of *Cromwell,* armies fright.
As long as rivers to the seas shall run,
As long as Cynthia shall relieve the sun,
While stags shall fly unto the forests thick,
While sheep delight the grassy downs to pick,
As long as future times succeeds the past,
Always thy honour, praise, and name shall last.

Thou in a pitch how far beyond the sphere
Of human glory tower'st, and reigning there
Despoiled of mortal robes, in seas of bliss,
Plunging dost bathe, and tread the bright abyss:
There thy great soul yet once a world does see,
Spacious enough, and pure enough for thee.
How soon thou Moses hast, and Joshua found,
And David for the sword and harp renowned?
How straight canst to each happy mansion go?
(Far better known above than here below)
And in those joys dost spend the endless day,
Which in expressing we ourselves betray.

For we, since thou art gone, with heavy doom,
Wander like ghosts about thy lovèd tomb;
And lost in tears, have neither sight nor mind
To guide us upward through this region blind.
Since thou art gone, who best that way couldst teach,
Only our sighs, perhaps, may thither reach.

And Richard yet, where his great parent led,
Beats on the rugged track: he, virtue dead,
Revives, and by his milder beams assures;
And yet how much of them his grief obscures?

He, as his father, long was kept from sight
In private, to be viewed by better light;

But opened once, what splendour does he throw?
A Cromwell in an hour a prince will grow.
How he becomes that seat, how strongly strains,
How gently winds at once the ruling reins?
Heaven to this choice prepared a diadem,
Richer than any Eastern silk or gem;
A pearly rainbow, where the sun enchased
His brows, like an imperial jewel graced.
  We find already what those omens mean,
Earth ne'er more glad, nor heaven more serene.
Cease now our griefs, calm peace succeeds a war,
Rainbows to storms, Richard to Oliver.
Tempt not his clemency to try his power,
He threats no deluge, yet foretells a shower.

On Mr. Milton's 'Paradise Lost'

When I beheld the poet blind, yet bold,
In slender book his vast design unfold,
Messiah crowned, God's reconciled decree,
Rebelling Angels, the Forbidden Tree,
Heaven, Hell, Earth, Chaos, all; the argument
Held me a while, misdoubting his intent
That he would ruin (for I saw him strong)
The sacred truths to fable and old song,
(So Sampson groped the temple's posts in spite)
The world o'erwhelming to revenge his sight.
  Yet as I read, soon growing less severe,
I liked his project, the success did fear;
Through that wide field how he his way should find
O'er which lame faith leads understanding blind;
Lest he perplexed the things he would explain,
And what was easy he should render vain.

Or if a work so infinite he spanned,
Jealous I was that some less skilful hand
(Such as disquiet always what is well,
And by ill imitating would excel)
Might hence presume the whole Creation's day
To change in scenes, and show it in a play.

Pardon me, Mighty Poet, nor despise
My causeless, yet not impious, surmise.
But I am now convinced that none will dare
Within thy labours to pretend a share.
Thou hast not missed one thought that could be fit,
And all that was improper dost omit:
So that no room is here for writers left,
But to detect their ignorance or theft.
That majesty which through thy work doth reign
Draws the devout, deterring the profane.
And things divine thou treat'st of in such state
As them preserves, and thee, inviolate.
At once delight and horror on us seize,
Thou sing'st with so much gravity and ease;
And above human flight dost soar aloft,
With plume so strong, so equal, and so soft.
The bird named from that paradise you sing
So never flags, but always keeps on wing.

Where couldst thou words of such a compass find?
Whence furnish such a vast expense of mind?
Just heaven thee, like Tiresias, to requite,
Rewards with prophecy thy loss of sight.

Well mightst thou scorn thy readers to allure
With tinkling rhyme, of thine own sense secure;
While the *Town-Bayes* writes all the while and spells,
And like a pack-horse tires without his bells.
Their fancies like our bushy points appear,
The poets tag them; we for fashion wear.

I too, transported by the mode, offend,
And while I meant to *praise* thee must *commend*.
Thy verse created like thy theme sublime,
In number, weight, and measure, needs not rhyme.

Notes

The poems are arranged as closely to the chronological order of composition as we can establish. This chronology is not to be trusted.

A Dialogue between Thyrsis and Dorinda. William Lawes set this poem.

Flecknoe, an English Priest at Rome. John Dryden probably wrote "Mac Flecknoe" in 1678. Line 4, "Lord Brooke" is the poet Fulke Greville.

Upon the Death of the Lord Hastings. Lord Hastings died in 1649. The collection of memorial verses also included work by Robert Herrick, Charles Cotton, John Denham, and John Dryden.

To His Coy Mistress. Lines 33 and 44. In her edition, Elizabeth Story Donno substitutes "glue" for "hue" and "grates" for "gates," and supplies lucid arguments for her decisions. I restore the words commonly printed—for which there are also arguments—for familiarity's sake.

An Horatian Ode upon Cromwell's Return from Ireland. Cromwell returned in May 1650.

Tom May's Death. Ben Jonson had been May's mentor.

Upon Appleton House. It was here, at an estate belonging to Lord Fairfax, that Marvell tutored Fairfax's 12-year-old daughter.

The Garden. Marvell wrote a Latin poem called "Hortus," which is either an original draft of "The Garden" or a translation—but it is not identical.

Bermudas. We assume that Marvell wrote "Bermudas" while he tutored Cromwell's ward William Dutton, because Marvell then lived in the house of John Oxenbridge, who had visited Bermuda twice.

A Poem upon the Death of His Late Highness the Lord Protector. Cromwell died September 3, 1658.

On Mr. Milton's 'Paradise Lost.' This is the latest poem that we can date with any probability: early summer, 1674.

About the Editor

❖❖

Donald Hall was born in Connecticut in 1928 and lives on a family farm in New Hampshire where he free-lances, writing magazine articles, children's books, memoirs, textbooks, plays, criticism, short stories, and biographies. He has collected four volumes of essays about poetry, of which the most recent is Poetry and Ambition *(1988). His ten books of poems include* Kicking the Leaves *(1978),* The Happy Man *(1986),* The One Day *(1988), which won the National Book Critics Circle award, and* Old and New Poems *(1990).*